Pocket/
Technical

CU00673679

Architectu

The application of good acoustic design can seem daunting to designers when trying to understand the often-complex physics of sound control. The ever-increasing number of standards and performance criteria that can be requested on new developments further complicates acoustics for architects.

Architectural Acoustics, part of the *PocketArchitecture* series, provides the fundamental theory and understanding of acoustics and applications of effective detailing for specific building types and conditions in an accessible and clear technical guide.

The book provides:

■ a compact and understandable introduction to the fundamentals of building and architectural acoustics
■ definitions of suitable acoustic performance criteria for a wide range of common buildings and room types
■ guidance on specification and detailing of the most suitable construction types in North America and the UK.

This book is both a handy rule of thumb on acoustics for anyone involved in the design or construction of buildings, and an essential addition to any architect's reference library.

Ana M. Jaramillo holds a BSc in Architecture (2003), an MS in Architectural Acoustics (2005), and a PhD in Architecture (2013). Her previous roles include: Acoustical Consultant (2003–2008); Acoustics Professor and Researcher at the Instituto Tecnologico Metropolitano in Medellin, Colombia (2006–2008); and Instructor at Virginia Tech, USA (2012). Ana currently works for AFMG in North America.

Chris Steel, BSc (Hons), MPhil, MIOA, ICIOB, is Senior Acoustic Consultant at the Robin Mackenzie Partnership and Senior Research Fellow at Edinburgh Napier University, UK, focusing on building and environmental acoustics. Chris also lectures to MSc students on architectural acoustics and is a tutor for the Institute of Acoustics Diploma in Acoustics.

PocketArchitecture:
Technical Design Series

Series Editor: Ryan E. Smith

Building Information Modeling
Karen M. Kensek

Life Cycle Assessment
Kathrina Simonen

Daylighting and Integrated Lighting Design
Christopher Meek and Kevin Van Den Wymelenberg

Architectural Acoustics
Ana M. Jaramillo and Chris Steel

PocketArchitecture:
Technical Design Series

Architectural Acoustics

Ana M. Jaramillo and Chris Steel

Routledge
Taylor & Francis Group

LONDON AND NEW YORK

First published 2015
by Routledge
2 Park Square, Milton Park, Abingdon, Oxon OX14 4RN

and by Routledge
711 Third Avenue, New York, NY 10017

Routledge is an imprint of the Taylor & Francis Group, an informa business

British Library Cataloguing-in-Publication Data
A catalogue record for this book is available from the British Library

Library of Congress Cataloging-in-Publication Data
Jaramillo, A. M., 1979–
    Architectural acoustics / A.M. Jaramillo and C. Steel.
        pages cm. — (Pocketarchitecture : technical design series)
    Includes bibliographical references and index.
    1. Architectural acoustics. I. Steel, C., 1975- II. Title.
    NA2800.J37 2014
    729'.29—dc23   2014015304

ISBN: 978-0-415-73213-0 (hbk)
ISBN: 978-0-415-73214-7 (pbk)
ISBN: 978-1-315-75284-6 (ebk)

Typeset in Goudy and Univers
by Keystroke, Station Road, Codsall, Wolverhampton

Printed and bound in Great Britain by
TJ International Ltd, Padstow, Cornwall

Contents

Figures

Tables

Series Editor's Preface

Although architects and building professionals come into contact with, specify, design, and build technical practices every day, they actually know relatively little about them. They are "abstract systems" construed and constructed upon industry norms passed through generations of professionals. Most of them correct, but many, when disassociated with their cultural underpinnings of building vernacular and, more importantly, their scientific basis and practice contexts, present challenges that cause buildings to not perform as intended or worse lead to physical, economic, or social catastrophe.

PocketArchitecture: Technical Design Series fills this void. The series comprises succinct, easy to use, topic-based volumes that collate in one place unbiased, need-to-know technical information about specific subject areas by expert authors. This series demystifies technical design criteria and solutions. It presents information without overladen theory or anecdotal information. *PocketArchitecture* is on point.

As the name would suggest, the volumes in this series are pocket-sized and collectively serve as a knowledge base on technical subjects in architecture, creating a value-added information base for building novices and masters alike. In addition to architects, engineers, and contractors that deliver building projects, the series is appropriate for students and academics interested in accessible information on technical information as it relates to building design and construction.

Despite their size, the series volumes are highly illustrated. Furthermore, the volumes use easily accessible language to succinctly explain the fundamental concepts and then apply these basic ideas to cases of common issues encountered in the built environment. *PocketArchitecture* is essential, accessible, and authoritative. This makes it important reading for architectural technologists, architects, building surveyors, building commissioners, building engineers, other construction professionals, even owners and clients.

This volume, *Architectural Acoustics*, addresses a pithy non-visual building science subject that is often misunderstood by designers. The book is focused on developing a basic understanding of why acoustical design is important and provides rules of thumb for how to accomplish auditory optimization. Hearing greatly impacts our perception of the world and our experience of architectural space. Poor acoustical design has tangible social, environmental, and health implications that are not well understood by most architects. Knowledgeably designed acoustics can enhance the user function of architecture, and can improve our physical wellbeing. *Architectural Acoustics* provides the fundamental theory and understanding of acoustics and applications of effective detailing for specific building types and conditions in an accessible and clear technical guide.

Ryan E. Smith
Series Editor

Acknowledgments

Chris Steel would like to thank Lee Hadden and Lenka Kovacova for their invaluable contribution in the production of the technical drawings, Professor Sean Smith, Professor Sam Alwinkle, Dr. Dave Baker OBE, and Peter Wilson, for reviewing the initial proposal and some of the later chapters.

Ana Jaramillo would like to thank Ricardo and Amparo Jaramillo for being, as always, the first critical reviewers of the work.

Finally both authors would like to thank Ryan Smith for helping to set up and edit the final publication.

"The science of acoustics as applied to buildings is complex and, worse still for the architect, surveyor and engineer, often apparently counter-intuitive. *Architectural Acoustics* lifts the lid on the subject, clearly explaining the underlying principles and setting out useful and practical solutions for dealing with noise in all types of building. It should be the essential reference source for those involved in the design and delivery of new buildings and will be equally valuable to those working in the field of refurbishment and building alterations."

Dave Baker OBE, HonDEng, FRICS, FCIOB,
Chief Executive, Robust Details Limited, UK

Introduction

Architectural acoustics is a subject that is often overlooked by architects and designers, as it may be portrayed as esoteric or considered less important than other design requirements. When a project requires an acoustics report, design teams may ask, "Why are we doing this?" The truth is that good acoustic design is as much a key element of good building design as the consideration of lighting or thermal comfort. It is no exaggeration to state that almost every type of building can, and should, include some consideration of acoustics if the goal of the architect or designer is to create a building in which people feel comfortable and can function.

There can be very real social, economic, and environmental consequences when architects and designers fail to take cognizance of acoustics in buildings. Our hearing is a 24-hour, 360-degree field of experiences and as such impacts greatly our perception, even when we are sleeping; therefore, noise or unwanted sound can have a profound effect on the human body. The effects of even relatively low levels of noise can have a detrimental effect on our physical wellbeing. The World Health Organization considers noise to be a more likely contributor to poor health and early mortality than damp housing and indoor radon gas. Be assured, unnecessarily noisy environments can be a hazard to health but the issues associated with acoustic design go beyond just controlling very noisy environments such as commercial or industrial buildings.

The failure to provide good acoustic detailing when creating new offices for, say, a legal firm or doctors' practices can readily result in a problematic loss of confidentiality making the building unusable. An inability to fully understand the very particular acoustic performance parameters set by hotel or cinema chains will result in the very real risk of having to deal with a client who will refuse to take ownership of the building. Forget to consider noise breakout when working on a new restaurant or retail outlet, and don't be too surprised if the result is a temporary closure, resulting in mounting remedial costs and a substantial loss of earnings to the client. These are not just examples of theoretical outcomes; they are actual events that have happened to major well-known firms over the past two decades.

Good architectural acoustics should not, however, be seen as something we do just to avoid risk. It can just as easily result in significant rewards for the client, designer, and building users. Good architectural acoustics within teaching environments can help to improve the educational attainment of the students who use the building. The thoughtful acoustic design of hospital buildings has been shown to improve patient recovery times and even reduce medication requirements and readmittance rates. Good acoustic design in the workplace has been shown to improve office worker productivity and increase retail sales. All of these benefits are the result of the built environment created by the architect or designer, often with the help of an acoustics expert.

The application of good acoustic design can seem daunting when trying to understand the often-complex physics of sound control or negotiating the ever-expanding canon of acoustic performance requirements, but even with a basic understanding of architectural acoustics it is possible for the most obvious of mistakes to be avoided and good design to become second nature.

The purpose of this book is to provide the architect, designer, contractor, technician, or student with a basic understanding of architectural acoustics. To provide a working knowledge of how sound affects a building and how it is controlled. To highlight the key acoustic design features and targets in a range of building types while providing a toolkit of information that can be referred to whenever a new project is undertaken. We have attempted to keep the mathematical explanation of sound to a minimum and focus on a narrative explanation of acoustics. This book is designed for those looking for the practical rather than the theoretical; however, for those interested in a deeper understanding the core equations for buildings acoustics are included as Appendices to the main text and referenced where necessary.

The first part of the book assumes that the reader is coming to acoustics from a fresh perspective and so tries to explain the basic concepts in a concise manner, focusing on some of the key knowledge required in architectural acoustics. The second part focuses on the design of particular building types and, rather than showing case studies – which can often result in information which is project-specific – it provides a systematic guide to good design, highlighting the most common acoustic problems and offering guidance. The information in the second part of the book is bolstered by the technical specifications included in the Appendices, to allow for quick referencing.

PocketArchitecture: Architectural Acoustics hopes to provide the fundamental theory, practical application, and key design tools required for good acoustic design in an accessible and clear format.

Part I

Principles

chapter 1

Basic concepts

SOUND IS A PRESSURE DISTURBANCE in the form of a longitudinal wave that produces an auditory sensation. Because of this there are always two important parts of the analysis of sound: the source and the receiver. To understand the behavior of sound in buildings, we need to understand the basic physics of sound. In this section we will begin by defining the main characteristics of the sound wave. First, imagine sound as a dominoes effect. Each molecule is excited and triggers the one next to it, but the molecules remain in almost the same position they started. However, the effect has been carried along and you can say something is "traveling." In architectural acoustics we usually talk about sound traveling through air. This means that a small vibration has created a variation in the air pressure and molecules are beginning to move back and forth, carrying the energy. This energy is spent along the way and thus the level decreases with distance.

The simplest sound is a pure tone. This means that it is composed by only one frequency (tone) and it is represented as a sine wave. The peaks of the sine wave are the points of highest pressure.

1.1 Speed of sound [C]

SOUND NEEDS A MEDIUM TO PROPAGATE and it travels at different speeds depending on the medium. The more dense the medium, the faster sound will travel. For example, in steel, sound travels at 20,000 ft/s (6,100 m/s), while in air sound travels at approximately 1,125 ft/s (343 m/s). Did you ever wonder why someone would get down and put their ears to the railroad track instead of pointing their ears up toward the train? Well, they would detect the incoming train earlier through the steel than through the air. Sound speed varies depending on the temperature, density, and elasticity of the medium.

1.2 Sound pressure [P]

SOUND PRESSURE IS THE DIFFERENCE between the pressure of the sound wave and the pressure of the medium (usually air). It is very small compared to the atmospheric pressure and measured in Pascals [Pa].

Amplitude is the difference between the maximum and minimum sound pressures of the wave.

1.3 Frequency [f]

FREQUENCY IS THE NUMBER OF OSCILLATIONS per second of the sound wave. It is measured in Hertz [Hz] or cycles per second. This frequency corresponds directly with the mechanical vibration frequency of the sound source.

We have already mentioned that a sound can be composed of only one frequency: the pure tone. But most sounds we hear every day are a lot more complex than that. Sounds produced by musical instruments, for example, are not pure tones. They are composed by a number of tones (or harmonics) that are related to the main tone. Other sounds are more randomly composed of a multitude of frequencies. Sounds such as speech, the sound of a lawnmower, the static of a radio, are very hard to describe in terms of each frequency that is part of them. Because of this, frequencies are usually grouped for analysis and measurement. These groups are called frequency bands.

1.3.1 Bandwidth

The term "bandwidth" refers to how much of the frequency range is included in a specific sound or the analysis of a sound. "Broadband" usually refers to the entire audible frequency range, or most of it. "Narrow band," on the other hand, is commonly used to refer to single or very small groups of frequencies.

1.3.2 Frequency band

As mentioned above, frequencies are clustered in bands in order to make them easier to study and represent. The most common band is the octave. The term "octave" is borrowed from the music field, where it means the interval between one note in the scale and the same note in the next scale (Figure 1.1).

In acoustics, an octave is the distance or interval between a tone at any specific frequency and the tone which is twice that frequency; however, there

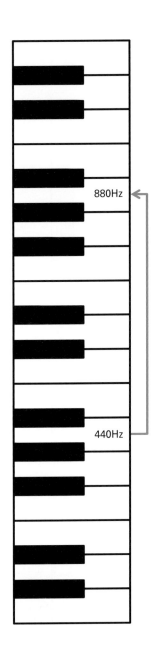

880Hz

440Hz

One octave = double the frequency

1.1 One octave in music and acoustics

50	
63	**63**
80	
100	
125	**125**
160	
200	
250	**250**
315	
400	
500	**500**
630	
800	
1000	**1000**
1250	
1600	
2000	**2000**
2500	
3150	
4000	**4000**
5000	
6300	
8000	**8000**
10000	

1.2 Octave and 1/3 octave bands

are some internationally accepted octave bands for the study of acoustics. They begin at 31.5 Hz and go up by doubling the frequency: 63 Hz, 125 Hz, 250 Hz and so on. These numbers correspond to the center of the frequency range covered by each band (e.g., the 1K octave band contains the frequencies between 707 and 1414 Hz). It is common to use smaller divisions of an octave for the study of acoustics, such as 1/3 or 1/12 of an octave (Figure 1.2).

1.3.3 Sound spectrum

Sound is commonly represented as a wave in time with amplitude in the Y axis; however, with the exception of the simplest sounds (composed by only one or two frequencies), this representation does not tell us much about how they "sound." We know from an energy-time chart how loud it was at different points of time, but we can't tell the pitch by looking at it, the way we could with a sine wave. In those cases we represent sound in terms of its amplitude and frequency. This is called a sound spectrum. In Figure 1.3, we have a spectrum by 1/3 octave bands.

A spectrum will give us a very good idea of how the sound was in terms of both its loudness and its pitch, but not how it varied in time. This is usually not necessary for short impulsive noise, or for long but steady noises. In some cases, though, we would need to use both graphical representations, because we need to understand amplitude and frequency as well as the changes over time (i.e., when measuring community ambient noise).

1.4 Period [T] and wavelength [λ]

PERIOD IS THE DURATION IN SECONDS [S] of one full cycle or oscillation on the wave.

Wavelength is the length of one full cycle. It is measured in distance units (meters, feet, inches, etc.). Wavelength, frequency, and the speed of sound are related by Eq. A.1. Higher frequencies have smaller wavelengths, and when we talk of architectural acoustics it is very important to understand the wavelength of sound. In the range of frequencies that are audible for the human ear, wavelengths are comparable in size to architectural elements – that is, they go from about 5/64 in (2 mm) to 65 ft (20 m) long. So, to be able to affect the way sound behaves in a room we have to understand its frequency content.

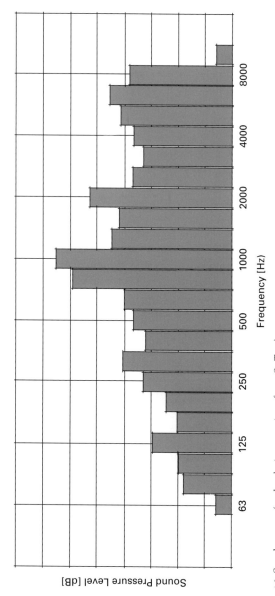

1.3 Sound spectrum (produced using measuring software SysTune)

Further reading

Egan, M. D. (1988). *Architectural acoustics*. New York: McGraw-Hill.

Jaramillo, A. M. (2007). *Acústica: La ciencia del sonido*. Medellín: Fondo Editorial ITM.

chapter 2

Interaction of sound
wave and medium

SOUND INTERACTS WITH MEDIA in many different ways. When a sound
wave strikes a wall, there is usually more than one phenomenon occurring to
it. This means the energy is distributed in different ways: part of the energy
might bounce back (reflection), part of the energy might go through (transmission), and part of the energy yet might be lost inside the material and
converted to heat (absorption) (Figure 2.1).

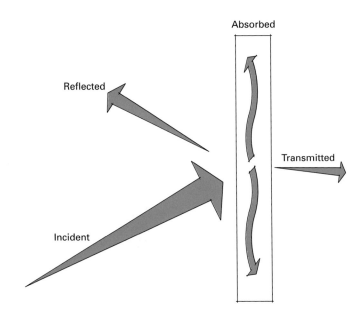

2.1 Incident wave's energy is being distributed between reflection, transmission, and absorption
phenomena

2.1 Reflection

REFLECTION OCCURS WHEN A SOUND WAVE striking an obstacle is redirected back to the space it came from in a specular manner, which is the way mirrors reflect light. The angle of incidence is the same as the angle of reflection (Figure 2.2).

In order for a wall to reflect sound, it needs to be dense, smooth, flat, and large. If one or more of these characteristics is missing, then there will be other phenomena occurring to the wave. The obstacle in the path of the wave needs to be dense in order to avoid the transmission of energy through it; it needs to be smooth in order to avoid the diffusion of energy in all directions; and it needs to be flat so the energy won't be either diffused or focalized and it needs to be large in order to avoid diffraction of the wave. This last characteristic is relative to frequency, which means the obstacle should be

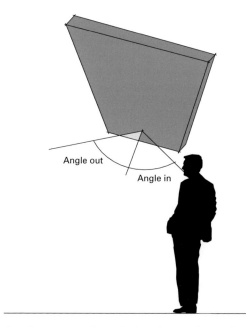

2.2 Angle of sound entering is equal to angle of sound exiting when panel is two to four times the size of the sound wave acting upon it

larger than the wavelength of the frequency it intends to reflect. The best way to understand the relationship between the wavelength and the ability of an obstacle to affect that wave is to imagine sound as water. If you want to stop the flow of a trickle of water you might use your hands. If you want to stop a small stream, maybe you'll have to use some small trees like a beaver would do. But if you try stopping the flow of the Amazon River with your hands or a small tree, it will just flow around you as if nothing was in its way.

2.1.1 Focalization

A very specific case of reflection of sound is when a large concave wall or ceiling is made of a reflective material. We know that for a specular reflection of sound the reflecting wall needs to be flat, and that a convex wall will diffuse the sound energy in multiple directions. When sound strikes a concave wall, the opposite occurs: a focal point exists where all reflections of sound are concentrated. In Figure 2.3 a semicircle room was simulated and reflections of sound can be seen arriving at a focal point. In this case, the curved wall is actually simulated as a sequence of straight walls so the focal point is somewhat larger than for a true circular shape.

The use of concave walls is not necessarily something that needs to be avoided as long as this phenomenon is taken into account. A very flat curve on a ceiling could be used positioning the focal point outside and far from

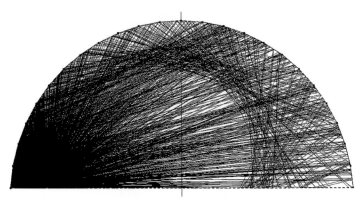

2.3 Focalization of sound reflections due to a concave wall (simulation created using the software EASE)

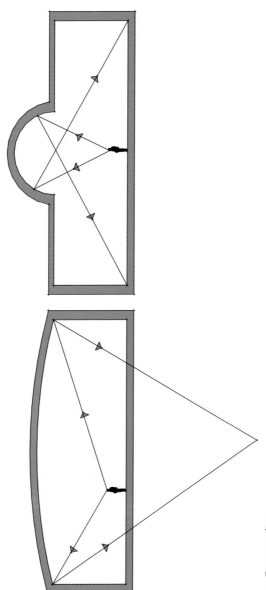

2.4 Concave ceilings

the listening space (Figure 2.4). The opposite is also true: a very small radius curve can be used if the focal point is not located in the intended audience area.

2.2 Diffraction

DIFFRACTION OCCURS WHEN A SOUND WAVE changes direction due to a change of medium, or an obstacle of a similar size to the wavelength. This phenomenon is very important in the design of noise barriers. The noise shadow area created by the barrier would not be the same as the shadow created by light hitting it. Due to the larger wavelength of sound, it will actually bend around the barrier and continue to travel (Figure 2.5).

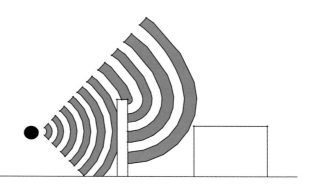

2.5 Diffraction of noise around a barrier

2.3 Scattering

WHEN A SOUND WAVE STRIKES A WALL that is not smooth or flat, then the incident energy won't be reflected specularly. This means that the energy will instead be scattered in multiple directions. Scattering can occur on a very specific diffusion pattern if the surface is convex or mathematically designed, or randomly if the surface has a texture in its material or construction (Figure 2.6).

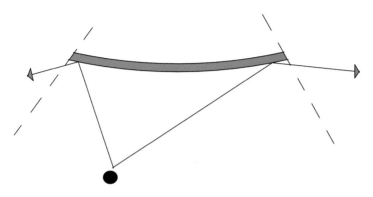

2.6 Sound wave scattered in multiple directions due to a convex surface

2.4 Transmission

SOUND TRANSMISSION THROUGH A STRUCTURE is the passage of the sound pressure wave from the air, into the structure, through the structure and then out the other side. During this process some of the sound pressure is reflected back into the room while some is lost within the structure of the wall (Figure 2.7).

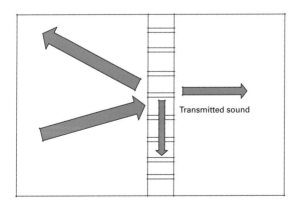

Transmitted sound

2.7 Basic sound transmission

If a 60 dB sound strikes a wall and 20 dB are measured on the other side of the partition, we say that the wall has 40 dB of transmission loss. This number, as you might have guessed, is different at every frequency. Eq. A.12 details how sound transmission is calculated. Low frequency noise pushes the whole structure causing the sound pressure wave to be transmitted by the surface of the wall or floor. At higher frequencies, sound can also find transmission paths through structural connections or by causing components or sections of the partition to resonate or vibrate. Finally sound will also transmit through small gaps or voids within the structure or through weaker flanking elements such as adjoining walls or service runs.

All of these frequencies are transmitted at the same time, so that a partition or a panel will be vibrating at different frequencies and in different planes. One way to visualize what is happening is to think of the surface of the sea on a stormy day. The swell of the sea, the slow rise and fall, is like the low frequency sound waves with the smaller choppy surface waves and ripples akin to the mid and higher frequency respectively.

2.4.1 Basic mechanisms for controlling sound transmission

There are eight key factors in the reduction of sound through a building structure:

- stiffness
- resonance
- isolation
- mass
- absorption
- critical frequency
- completeness
- flanking transmission.

Stiffness of a structure The stiffness of a partition particularly affects sound transmission at low frequencies. Stiff materials will naturally resist any force against it, such as a sound wave, and the greater the stiffness or rigidity, the better a material will be at reducing the transmission of lower frequency sound.

Cast in-situ concrete decks can provide very high levels of acoustic insulation between floors despite the apparently slim section of concrete slab.

The profiles, while adding mass to the structure, also act as stiffeners to the floor structure and so performance levels are better than may be expected from a simple thin slab of a similar thickness (Figure 2.8). Increased dwangs/noggins or strutting/blocking in a timber floor help improve the stiffness of a floor. Similarly timber floors with heavy deafening or pugging also help to improve stiffness in the floor as well as mass.

Resonance The beneficial effects of stiffness are limited. One of the first limiting factors is that all materials have a natural resonance frequency. A frequency at which a material or structure stops acting like a stiff element and starts to naturally vibrate, similar to the natural ring of a bell when struck.

As the sound wave pushes against the surface of a material, there are frequencies at which it is easier for the sound wave to excite the surface of the material. This is similar to the effect you would get when pushing a child on a swing. There is a "sweet spot" where you no longer have to exert any great amount of energy to keep the swing in motion. The destruction of the Tacoma Narrows Bridge or the Wobbly Millennium Bridge in London are extreme examples of what happens when a structure is excited at its natural or resonance frequency.

With wall and floor structures, the more similarity there is in the structure the easier it is for resonance to occur, e.g., solid homogenous walls. Therefore it can be beneficial to the sound insulation of a structure if symmetry in the construction can be avoided, e.g., lining one side of a brick wall with a metal stud and plasterboard.

Where the benefits of stiffness give way to resonance effects, there is a drop in acoustic performance. This may to occur outside the 100 Hz to 3150 Hz frequency range over which sound insulation is commonly measured; however, it has an effect on the overall performance, as it can effectively lower the starting point at which the structure starts to recover. The closer this occurs to the 100 Hz frequency, the greater the effect it will have on the acoustic performance.

Figure 2.9 shows the expected resonance dip from a double-thick brick wall and a twin-leaf-thick brick wall. In both instances the amount of material used is the same, two layers of brick, but the wall with the cavity has a lower resonance frequency and so the dip occurs at a lower frequency along the X axis. This is as a result of isolation creating a mass-spring-mass effect, where the cavity acts like a spring layer dampening the forced transmission of

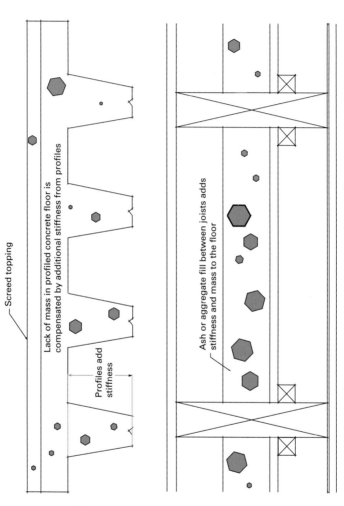

Screed topping

Lack of mass in profiled concrete floor is compensated by additional stiffness from profiles

Profiles add stiffness

Ash or aggregate fill between joists adds stiffness and mass to the floor

2.8 Profiles in concrete decks or heavy mass materials between joists improve stiffness

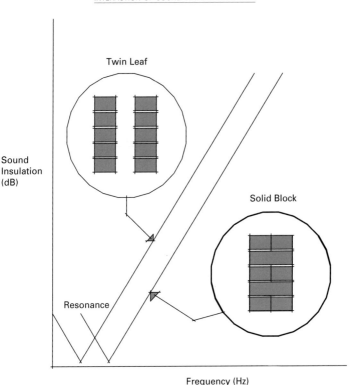

2.9 Resonance dip of two walls with the same mass but different constructions

sound from one leaf to the next. If the two lines were laid on top of each other, they would describe the same path, but because of that lower dip in performance the twin-leaf wall gains improvement across the higher frequency range. We have simply moved the resonance frequency back by introducing the cavity.

These constructions also benefit physical isolation, with the thickness and mass of each wall system dictating performance as shown in Eq. A.14.

Isolation of a structure Isolation is the primary means by which twin-leaf partitions, suspended ceiling systems, and floating floors improve the acoustic performance of a wall or floor. Figure 2.10 provides an outline of how the isolation of a solid wall with the application of a free standing partition can improve sound insulation.

Isolation is particularly important for the acoustic insulation of floors against impact sound. Impact resistant mats, isolated floor battens, and floating floor systems all help to isolate a structure from impact sound. They will also have an effect on the transmission of airborne sound, as will twin-stud or twin-leaf wall systems, or independent ceiling or wall lining systems. Finally, the more materials sound has to transmit though, the more energy is lost and so isolation helps with this process by adding different materials and creating cavities in a floor or wall structure.

1   No isolation allows for the lower frequency sound to directly interact with the wall. Here, the natural resonance of a partition is the driving factor.
2   Introducing an isolation layer creates the mass-spring-mass effect.
3   As we move up the frequency range, the wavelength of the sound gets shorter and so, instead of being able to force the whole partition into motion, the sound finds paths through the structure.
4   By separating (or isolating) the different elements of the structure, we break the structural paths that allow for sound transmission at mid- to high frequencies.

(see Figure 2.10)

Mass of a structure   The more mass a material or structure has, the more difficulty the sound pressure wave has in forcing it into vibration. For most materials mass is the defining factor in acoustic transmission performance. For every doubling of mass in a structure or material, we should see a 6 dB improvement in acoustic insulation. However, this will only be noticed at the mass-controlled frequencies. This normally occurs at the mid-range of frequencies and can be calculated using the mass law Eq. A.15.

The reason why some single-leaf brick walls can provide similar levels of acoustic insulation to a metal or timber stud partition with multiple linings is the substitution of isolation (e.g., the isolation of the two plasterboard layers by the frame) for increased mass (the inherent mass of the brick or block work).

Absorption within a structure   Within a structure, absorption occurs (to some extent) within the materials, but also within any cavity. Adding absorptive

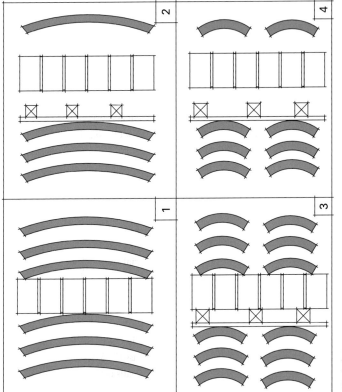

2.10 Isolation

materials to the cavities within a partition, we can improve the effects of absorption within the cavity by placing a material that is more efficient at absorbing sound than just air. This is normally achieved by adding porous materials such as mineral fiber, glass fiber, open cell foams, or even natural fibrous materials (e.g., sheep's wool). As a general rule, materials with a density of 0.62–2.25 lb/ft³ (10–36 kg/m³) are best at absorbing sound in a partition cavity. The inclusion of such materials can improve the acoustic insulation of a partition by 3–6

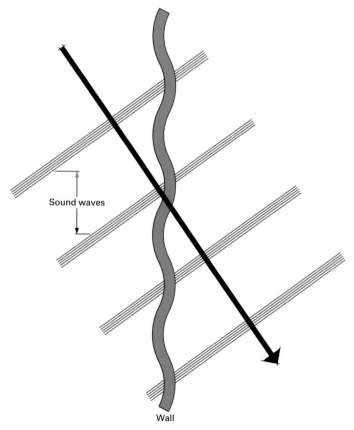

Sound waves

Wall

2.11 Critical frequency or the coincidence effect where grazing sound waves coincided with the surface waves on a panel

dB. The principles of absorption within a cavity are the same as the principles for absorption within a space and further detail on absorption can be found in Section 2.5.

Critical frequency The critical frequency is also known as the coincidence effect. The coincidence effect occurs when the length of a sound wave grazing against the surface of a material coincides with the natural bending waves on the surface of a panel. Effectively the speed of the sound through the air does not have to slow down when it passes through the material and so the material becomes acoustically transparent, as shown in Figure 2.11.

This is seen as a dip or leveling out in performance at frequencies above the mass controlled region. The thicker a material, the lower the critical frequency becomes and the more likely it will occur within the frequencies of interest for sound insulation. They are normally easy to distinguish in lightweight plasterboard partitions, as they tend to occur at around 2000 Hz, which is around the critical frequency for plasterboard. Using double layers of plasterboard that have differing thickness and mass can help reduce this effect, as can avoiding symmetry in a wall system. The critical frequency can be calculated using Eq. A.16.

Completeness of a structure Without a complete structure, sound can leak through any gaps or holes in the same way that water would leak through the cracks in a dam. In addition to gaps or holes in constructions, incompleteness of a structure or weaknesses in a structure will also have a similar effect. Common reasons for poor sound insulation from incomplete structures are:

- lack of architectural detailing for wall heads or service penetrations
- failing to instruct which contractor is responsible for detailing of wall heads and service penetrations
- missing materials within a wall or floor structure, such as failing to place absorptive layers within cavities or the coring out of screeds and mass elements for services
- poor workmanship.

Flanking sound affecting a structure Sound always takes the path of least resistance. Flanking sound transmission relates to noise that is transmitted into an adjoining room or space but which does not come directly through the separating partition. It is possible for there to be at least 12 possible flanking transmission paths between two rooms separated by a simple wall construction (flanking via the side walls, floor, and ceiling). Direct sound is controlled by the wall (Figure 2.12, item 1), while the surrounding structure controls flanking (Figure 2.12, items 2) either directly through flanking structures or even through flanking structures and back into the separating wall.

1   Direct sound transmission.
2   Flanking paths for a simple separating wall.

(see Figure 2.12)

Flanking transmission paths can be controlled by ensuring that the separating wall or floor is built into the flanking walls (e.g., build block work separating walls or pre-cast concrete slabs so they break the flanking wall) or line flanking walls with isolated frames, such as is common in timber kit constructions (Figure 2.13).

1   Untreated flanking wall allows for transmission of sound.
2   Separating wall is built into flanking wall to help reduce the structural transmission path. It can be fully built in or toothed in block work coursings. Fully built, it is more effective.
3   Independent linings either side of the separating wall help to control flanking transmission.

(see Figure 2.13, page 26)

Note: The higher the performance requirement of the partition, the greater level of flanking detail is required.

Flanking transmission can be a particular problem with masonry-supported timber floors where there is a strong structural connection between rooms due to continuous masonry walls running up through a building. It is generally recommended that such constructions are avoided for floors where performance levels of above STC/R_w 55 dB are required.

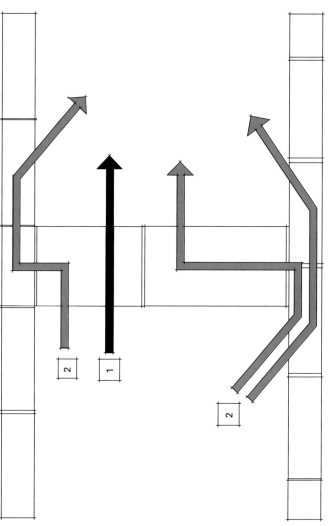

2.12 Flanking transmission paths

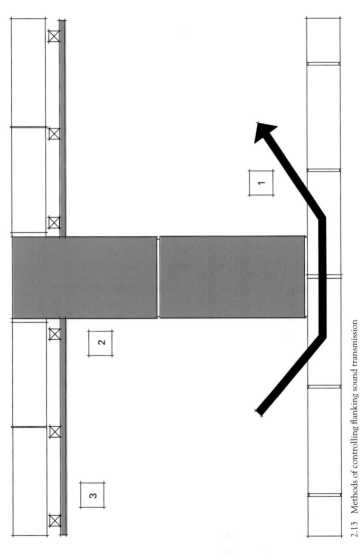

2.13 Methods of controlling flanking sound transmission

2.4.2 The difference between and plasterboard stud partitions

Block work or concrete walls or floors depend on structural mass for good acoustics and tend to provide good insulation at low frequencies. Good performance can also be achieved at high frequencies if the partition is well sealed (e.g., parge coats on block work walls or cast in-situ concrete slabs). These structures tend to have very rigid connections, so isolation for impact sound should always be considered for concrete floors, although soft floor coverings can often provide more than enough control.

Timber separating floors/walls or metal stud partitions depend on isolation of the structural elements for their performance. They tend to have poorer levels of performance at low frequencies and the only way to reduce this effect is to provide larger cavities between linings (i.e., deeper wall and floor sections). They tend to provide good levels of sound insulation at higher frequencies, due to the inherent separation of the flanking structure and the overall completeness of the partition type. With good isolation detailing, timber floor structures can provide good performance against impact sound. The presence of open cavities within the structure should also be seen as an opportunity to introduce acoustically absorptive layers to help further reduce sound transmission.

2.5 Absorption

ALL MATERIALS WILL ABSORB some sound that comes into contact with it. As a sound wave impacts onto a surface, some of the energy is reflected back, some is transmitted through the material, and some is lost within the material itself. The harder, heavier, and smoother a material is, the poorer it will be at absorbing sound. The only exception to this rule comes in the form of panel absorbers. Finishes such as glass or brick are poor at absorbing sound, while finishes such as soft, unvarnished timbers are better and mineral or glass fiber ceiling tiles are very good. Table 2.1 shows some common materials ranked in order of how well they absorb sound.

The Noise Reduction Coefficient (NRC), used in North America, or the average absorption coefficient (α_w), used in Europe, define how good a material is at absorbing sound. The closer the material is to 1, the more sound it absorbs.

There are databases available which detail the acoustic absorption of a range of building materials, finishes, and even items of furniture. Appendix C

Table 2.1 Acoustic absorption of materials ranked by performance

Material	NRC	Performance
Marble	0	Almost completely reflective
Plastered block work	0.05	Very poor absorption
Window	0.15	Low absorption
Carpet on rubber underlay	0.55	Good absorption
Mineral fiber ceiling tile with quilt overlay	0.95	Almost completely absorptive

includes two tables showing typical performance values of a range of materials, but it is worth seeking measurement data from manufacturers on a project-by-project basis.

2.5.1 Porous absorbers, panel absorbers, and composite absorbers

Acoustically absorptive materials commonly used in architecture fall into three main categories:

A   Porous absorber
B   Panel absorber
C   Composite absorber   (see Figure 2.14)

Porous absorbers are materials such as mineral fiber ceiling tiles, carpets, curtains or open cell foam panels. Here sound waves come into contact with the material and the energy in the sound wave is transferred into the porous material. The sound wave causes friction within the porous or fibrous structure of the material thereby changing the sound wave energy into heat. Acoustic energy is lost and the sound wave being reflected is weaker. Porous or fibrous absorbers are commonly good at absorbing sound across a wide range of frequencies.

Panel absorbers are made of a thin panel that is set off a wall or ceiling surface and the depth of the cavity behind the panel, along with the overall mass of the panel, determines the frequency at which most sound is absorbed (see Figure A.2 and Eq. A.20). As sound hits the panel, some is transmitted through into the cavity and this sound is then reflected off the wall or ceiling and back toward the panel. The sound wave passing through

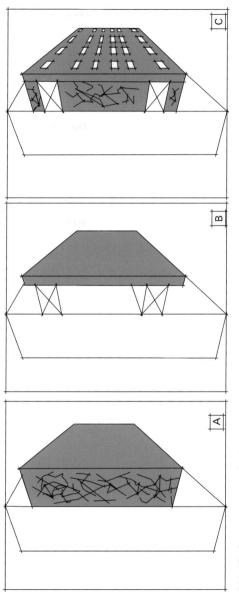

2.14 The three most common absorber types

the panel causes it to vibrate and, by setting the panel a particular distance from the wall, it is possible to have the panel vibrate with the sound wave being reflected off the wall. Two wave fronts which are out of phase but vibrating at the same speed will tend to cause a canceling effect whether they are sound in the air or waves in the sea. Solid panel absorbers are better at controlling reverberation at lower frequencies, although the lower the frequency, the further the panel would have to be set from the wall. They are also more effective around a narrow band of frequencies.

Resonant absorbers, also called cavity absorbers, work like an empty bottle when you blow a constant column of air at the opening and it produces one tone (see Figure A.3 and Eq. A.21). The only way to change that tone is to change the volume of the cavity by filling it partly with water. Resonant absorbers are then a single or a group of "recipients" that are tuned to absorb a single frequency.

Composite panel/porous absorbers are a mix between the previous categories. A panel absorber is enhanced by introducing an acoustically porous material in the cavity created by the panel and the wall. The panel is usually also given perforations or slots which allow sound waves to be better absorbed by the fill material as well as having a Helmholtz effect (resonance) where the perforations or slots allow for absorption. The greater the number of slots or holes, the better the panel will work at higher frequencies. These composite absorbers can provide good performance across a range of frequencies.

A   Porous absorbers work at a wide range of frequencies.
B   Panel and resonant absorbers work at a narrow range of frequencies but perform better.
C   Composite absorbers widen the range of panel or resonant absorbers but lower performance at the design frequency.

(see Figure 2.15)

2.5.2 Effects of material properties of absorbers

Alterations to the material properties of an acoustic absorber can affect how it will perform.

For porous materials, the following rules can be applied:

■   The deeper the panel, the better it will perform at low frequencies and so enhance performance across the frequency range. Some of this performance can be obtained by separating the panel from the wall.

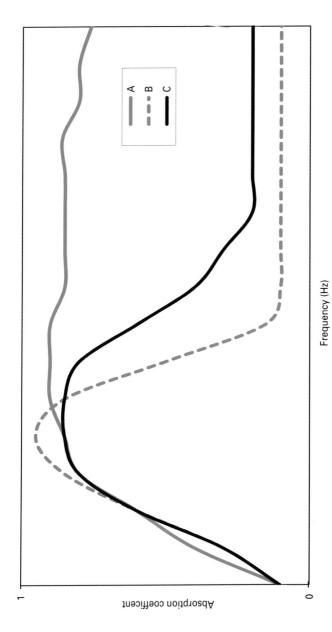

2.15 Acoustic absorbers and their frequency performance

- Densities of between 0.62 and 2.06 lb/ft³ (10 and 33 kg/m³) tend to absorb sound more efficiently.
- Larger panel sizes will be more effective at absorbing low frequency sound.
- For porous materials, achieving effects below 100 Hz is likely to result in impractically thick panels.

For panel absorbers, the following rules can be applied:

- Where thinner panel materials are used, performances at lower frequencies will be improved; thicker panels will be more effective at absorbing higher frequencies.
- Increasing the distance the panel is set from the wall will result in better performance at lower frequencies. Shallower depths will absorb higher frequencies better.
- Increasing dampening of the panel, e.g., laminated materials, will help absorb sound across a wider frequency band.

For composite panel absorbers with porous backings and perforations/slots, the following rules can be applied:

- The rules specific to the properties of the porous material and panel, given in the two preceding sections, will apply.
- Perforations ratios of 15 percent are sufficient for thin panels, but this should be increased if the panel thickness increases (30 percent perforations are common).
- It is better to perforate with many small holes than with a small number of large holes.

2.5.3 Rating acoustic absorbers

Some acoustic absorbers are good across a frequency range, some better at specific frequencies, but all are rated against either the Noise Reduction or Absorption Coefficient. In Europe, categorizations from A (highly absorptive materials) through E (very little absorption) are used (BS EN ISO 11654 1997) and broadly fall into the categories shown in Table 2.2.

Highly absorptive materials such as mineral fiber will have absorption coefficients of around 0.9 (1.0 being around 100 percent absorptive). It

Table 2.2 **Absorption performance levels (BS EN ISO 11654:1997)**

Absorption classification	Panel absorbers	Porous absorbers
	Minimum average αw between 250 Hz and 2 kHz	Minimum performance at each 1/3 Octave Band
A	0.90 to 1.00	>0.7 @ 250 Hz >0.9 @ 500 Hz to 2 kHz >0.8 @ 4 kHz
B	0.80 to 0.85	>0.6 @ 250 Hz >0.8 @ 500 Hz to 2 kHz >0.7 @4 kHz
C	0.60 to 0.75	>0.4 @ 250 Hz >0.6 @ 500 Hz to 2 kHz >0.5 @4 kHz
D	0.30 to 0.55	>0.1 @ 250 Hz >0.3 @ 500 Hz to 2 kHz >0.2 @4 kHz
E	0.25 to 0.15	>0.0 @ 250 Hz >0.1 @500 Hz to 2 KHz >0.05 @4 kHz

is unusual to see materials with absorption coefficients of above 1.0, as this would suggest that they are more than 100 percent absorptive.

In North America, it is common to use the Noise Reduction Coefficient (NRC) to rate absorbers, which is a simple average of the absorption coefficient at the mid-frequency octave bands:

$$\text{NRC} = \frac{\alpha_{250\,Hz} + \alpha_{500\,Hz} + \alpha_{1\,KHz} + \alpha_{2\,KHz}}{4}$$

Because this single number does not give a clear idea of the properties of the material at the full frequency range, it is only used commercially. For specific calculations or design decisions, it is recommended to look for specific frequency band absorption coefficients.

2.5.4 Perceived impact of absorption

Adding or reducing the amount of absorption within a room will affect the reverberation or echo within the space, and it is common to alter the specification of particular surfaces or materials. In subsequent chapters, guidelines will be given on recommended surface areas of absorptive materials that should be added to particular types of rooms, to allow for target reverberation times to be achieved.

To achieve significant differences in perception, significant increases in absorption are required, i.e., entire wall, floor, or ceiling finishes may need to be altered.

Controlling reverberation also has an effect on the overall noise level within a room. By increasing the absorption in a space, we can reduce the overall noise level within a room. This can be of value when dealing with noise control in high noise environments such as factories. The reduction in overall noise levels is linked directly to the volume of the space. Figure 2.16 details the expected reductions in overall noise levels within a room due to additional absorption.

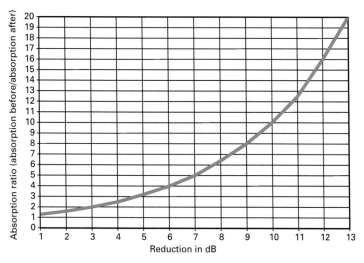

2.16   Noise reduction as a function of increasing absorption

Further reading

British Standards Institution (BSI) (1997) *Acoustics. Sound absorbers for use in buildings. Rating of sound absorption* (BS EN ISO 11654:1997). London: BSI.

Brüel & Kjær (1982) *Noise control, principles and practice*. Nærum, Denmark: Brüel & Kjær.

International Organization for Standards (ISO) (2012) *Acoustics – Measurement of room acoustic parameters – Part 3: Open plan offices* (EN ISO 3382-3 2012). Geneva, Switzerland: ISO.

chapter 3

Human hearing

3.1 Sound perception

HUMAN EARS ARE SENSITIVE TO SOUND in different degrees along the frequency range. We are most sensitive to mid-frequencies and it is not surprising that our ears are built to better understand sound in the range that we talk. The sensitivity to different frequencies also varies by the sound pressure level. As the level increases the differences flatten out. Figure 3.1 shows the human hearing range, from threshold of audibility to threshold of pain.

The human hearing range goes from approximately 20 Hz to 20,000 Hz. Below and above that range sound is inaudible for humans, but it might be audible for some animals, for example, the frequency used by bats to locate themselves (echolocation) or the frequency used for dog whistles.

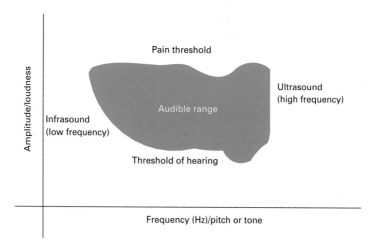

3.1 Human audible range

Table 3.1 Permissible noise exposure in hours per day at a certain sound pressure level (OSHA 1919.95)

Duration per day	Sound pressure level (slow response)
h:mm	dBA
8:00	90
6:00	92
4:00	95
3:00	97
2:00	100
1:30	102
1:00	105
0:30	110
0:15 or less	115

Humans also have an audible range of amplitudes that goes from very faint around 0 dB to painful at about 130 dB. Above the threshold of pain, our ears can be damaged permanently in a matter of seconds. Long exposures at lower amplitudes can also be damaging to our ears. Table 3.1 contains the limit time exposure at each SPL level per day dictated by OSHA. *Note:* Permissible levels in Europe are more stringent, with 6 hours at 80dB, 2 hours at 95dB, or 45minutes at 90dB, being sufficiently high exposure times to trigger requirements for noise assessment and hearing protection.

3.2 Loudness

LOUDNESS IS THE SUBJECTIVE IMPRESSION of level (what we commonly call "the volume" of a sound). Our ears are created to respond differently to sound at different frequencies, so two sounds at the same pressure level will not necessarily have the same loudness to our ears.

3.2.1 Equal loudness contour

Figure 3.2 defines the loudness of a specific sound. Each curve is associated with a loudness, defined in Phon. It is easy to see that the shape of the curves corresponds with the threshold of audibility, becoming flatter as loudness increases. It can also be observed in the figure that the human ear has very

3.2 Equal loudness contours (based on ISO 226:2203)

low sensitivity at the low frequencies. For example, a pure tone at 31.5 Hz with 95 dB of amplitude will sound as loud to our ears as one at 500 Hz with 60 dB. Both are 50 Phons.

3.3 Binaural hearing

3.3.1 Localization

Thanks to the fact that humans possess binaural hearing (those without hearing disabilities, including deafness in one or both ears), we are capable of localizing sound. This ability equates to having three-dimensional sight, or the ability to see depth due to the fact that we also have two eyes. Our ears give us the ability to localize sound in the horizontal plane up to 1 degree of precision. What happens in the vertical plane, though?

Our ears are located on both sides of the head, making it difficult to locate sounds that come from an equidistant position to both ears. This process of comparing two different signals received by the two ears happens in the brain before we can point to the location of the source. The brain looks basically to two characteristics of those signals. Interaural Level Differences (ILD) refers to the difference in level between the two signals and it is produced by the shadowing effect of the head to the ear farthest from the source, as well as the slight drop in level from traveling farther. Interaural Time Differences (ITD) refers to that difference in arrival time to both ears. Even though we can't consciously say how different those signals are, or even perceive them as two different signals, our brain is capable of processing the differences and giving us an answer regarding location.

In the vertical plane, however, our brain uses frequency cues to localize sounds, and this phenomenon is not as effective as the ITDs and ILDs on the horizontal plane (Figure 3.3).

Going back to the comparison with our visual sense, we notice that our eyes get the illusion of fluid motion in an animation of as low as 20 frames per second. That means that our eyes cannot tell the difference between 50 millisecond (ms) periods. Now, sound travels at about 1,115 ft/s (340 m/s) and the difference between our ears would never be traveled in more than 1 ms. So, how can these very small differences allow us to have such precision in localizing sounds?

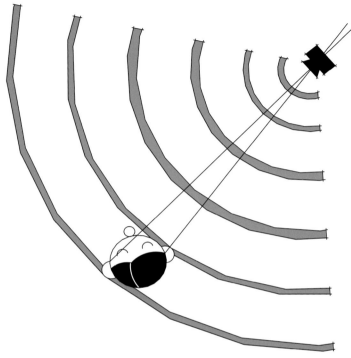

3.3 Binaural hearing

3.3.2 Precedence effect

Imagine a situation where sound is being played back through two loudspeakers located exactly at 45 degrees left and right in front of you. Your ears are both going to perceive exactly the same signal, because it is coming at equal times and at equal levels to them. Your brain, then, will conclude that there is only one loudspeaker located exactly in front of you. If we induced a delay of 40 ms in the left-side loudspeaker, we still cannot hear two signals, because the separation between them is not enough. However, our brain will identify the right side as the origin of sound and the left side as a reflection, thus localizing sound on the right side. Furthermore, if we raise the level of the left-side loudspeaker up to 10 dB, our brain will still be convinced of the origin of the signal being in the right side. These experiments were performed by Helmut

Hass, who arrived at the conclusion that ITDs are more defining to sound localization than ILDs, and so called it the precedence effect.

In real life we will always receive the direct sound before any reflection, and in most scenarios we will receive the direct sound at a higher level than the reflections. This is due to the fact that reflections will travel longer, losing some energy along the way, as well as part of their energy being absorbed by each obstacle they strike. There are rare cases, though, where the most direct path that the sound could take is blocked or shielded by an intervening structure. This means that a secondary sound path that may have reflected off another structure is the first sound we hear. As the reflected sound is now the dominant sound, we assume that this dictates the direction of the source. This is referred to as displacement, and requires that reflection to have a significant pressure level above the mitigated direct sound (Figure 3.4).

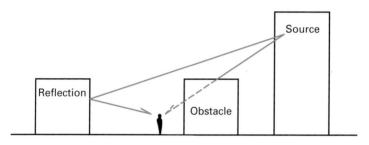

3.4 Displacement of the localization of the source

The sound will be perceived as arriving from the opposite direction, since the direct sound path is blocked.

Figure 3.5 (page 42) illustrates the following:

A   Reflections that come before 50 ms, and are significantly louder than the normal decay, could produce displacement of the source.

B   Reflections that come before 50 ms, and are at or below the normal decay, amplify the direct sound and reinforce the signal.

C   Reflections that come after 50 ms, and are significantly louder than the normal decay, are distinctly heard as echoes.

D   Reflections that come after 50 ms, and are at or below the normal decay, are reverberation.

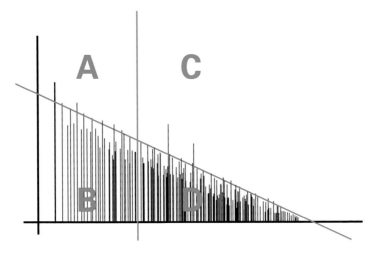

3.5 Reflectogram

Based on Figure 3.5, an **echo** (i.e., a distinct repetition of the signal) is a late reflection of sound that hasn't lost much energy (e.g., it only reflected once in a very reflective wall that is far away from the source). This is the reason why the back wall of venues is usually absorptive.

3.3.3 Cocktail party effect
Another effect that is enhanced by our binaural hearing is the cocktail party effect. This is our ability to discriminate one signal among many others, as in a cocktail party, where you can carry a conversation even though there are many others happening around you, and some of them louder. You can also decide to listen to another conversation that is happening in the room, and realize you can do it. A related phenomenon describes how your brain is "pulled" to hearing an unintended signal when something of particular interest to you is mentioned (e.g., your name), or how a non-native speaker is pulled by a conversation in his or her own native language that is happening in another part of the room.

3.4 Sound masking

IN THE ENVIRONMENTS WE INHABIT, there is always more than one sound arriving at our ears. We usually talk about signal and noise as a way of dividing those that we are interested in and those that we don't want. Noise is basically unwanted sound. But whether we want it or not, our brains are still processing all sound that arrives at our ears, and they will have an effect on what we finally *hear*.

Sounds have the ability to *mask* other sounds, especially if they are louder or lower in frequency. Sound masking can be a problem or a benefit, depending on how and where it happens.

If you are trying to have a conversation on the phone and the air conditioning kicks in with a loud rumble, you will probably experience unwanted masking. You realize that you have to make a bigger effort to hear the person on the other side of the line than you were doing so far. Now, imagine that you are sitting in a cubicle and the person in the next cubicle is having a conversation on the phone. When the air conditioning kicks in, it drowns the sound from their conversation and now it is easier for you to concentrate on your work. This would be desired masking.

Even though we strongly suggest that all background noise is undesirable, there are very specific cases where privacy is a priority and isolation between the people or groups of people is not possible, so a masking system is the solution to create privacy. This is very common in office environments, but it has also been implemented in hospital waiting rooms and other scenarios requiring privacy.

Further reading

Blauert, J. (1997) *Spatial hearing: The psychophysics of human sound localization.* Cambridge, MA: MIT.

Moray, N. (1959) Attention in dichotic listening: Affective cues and the influence of instructions. *Quarterly Journal of Experimental Psychology* 11(1): 56–60. doi:10.1080/17470215908416289.

chapter 4

Noise

4.1 External and internal performance criteria

THE WORLD HEALTH ORGANIZATION suggests external free-field levels of below $L_{Aeq\,(16hrs)}$ 50–55 dB as being suitable to avoid serious disturbance or annoyance during the daytime for dwellings, with more recent European guidelines suggesting maximum external free-field levels outside a dwelling of $L_{Aeq\,(8hours)}$ 40 dB as being suitable to avoid noise disturbance at night. However, in many instances (city center, some urban and suburban areas), a different approach may be suitable.

Table 4.1 defines some of the standard noise criteria applied in a range of cases. External noise is normally considered an issue for residential properties but can be a requirement for outdoor workspaces or education spaces. It should be noted that the requirements can differ greatly from country to country, state to state, and even from county to county.

Advice from the local authority should always be sought when designing for the control of external noise levels, particularly for dwellings.

Noise from entertainment sources (bars, clubs, pubs) is not normally required to be controlled outside the nearest residential property, as in most cases noise from these sources is associated with nighttime use and sleep disturbance within a property. Control levels for such noise will again differ from one area to another, so advice should always be sought, either when building dwellings next to an entertainment source or when introducing a new source of entertainment noise. Good practice guidelines on the design of commercial buildings are given in Chapter 13.

Table 4.1 Suitable external noise levels

Noise source and receiver description	Method of control	Performance criteria Upper noise level at the receptor
New industrial noise affecting existing residential properties or existing industrial affecting new residential	Noise levels should be controlled in relation to the pre-existing background noise level L_{A90} dB	−10 dB below the background = positive indication that complaints are unlikely Around +5 dB higher than the background level = moderate likelihood of disturbance +10 dB higher than the back ground level = likelihood of complaint significant
New office development mechanical noise affecting existing residential properties	Noise levels should be controlled in relation to an absolute level of noise that is frequency-specific	NR35 during the daytime NR25 during the nighttime NR20 for highly tonal or impulsive noise (e.g., electrical substations).
Construction noise affecting existing residential and commercial activities	Noise levels should be controlled to a maximum ambient level and operating times on site are restricted	$> L_{Aeq}$ 75 dB 8:00 a.m.–6:00 p.m. Monday– Friday 8:00 a.m.–12:00 p.m. Saturday Restricted activity at other times
Road, Rail,* affecting new residential developments	Noise levels should be controlled for private amenity spaces (e.g., rear gardens, balconies)	$>L_{Aeq}$ 55 dB 7:00 a.m.–11:00 p.m. $>L_{Aeq}$ 45 dB 11 p.m.–7:00 a.m.
Airport noise, affecting new residential developments	Noise levels should be controlled for private amenity spaces (e.g., rear gardens, balconies)	$>L_{Aeq}$ 57 dB 7:00 a.m.–11:00 p.m. $>L_{Aeq}$ 48 dB 11:00 p.m.–7:00 a.m.

Note:* For rail noise sources, it is also expected that during the nighttime period maximum individual noise events should not regularly exceed L_{Amax} 82 dB.

4.2 External noise control

4.2.1 Introduction

Almost any building that is proposed for an urban/suburban environment should take some account of the control of external noise. The ambient noise requirements set out in Appendix B are specification requirements intended to control this external noise and are an amalgamation of the current best practices issued in North America and Europe. In order to ensure that internal noise levels are achieved, it is necessary to understand the main design techniques used to control external noise. Table 4.2 outlines common noise levels that can be expected in a number of external environments.

4.2.2 Site development and screening

The chances of being able to select a site purely because it will be a quiet location are unlikely, as commercial and amenity requirements will always take precedence. This does not mean that site layouts cannot be developed to avoid additional cost to the building fabric or reduced usability.

When developing a site which is affected by noise, the following approach to design should be adopted:

■ For mixed use sites (e.g., residential with commercial), separate residential areas from existing noisy areas. Using office or commercial development

Table 4.2 Likely external ambient noise levels during the day (adapted from BS8233, 1999)

Source	A-weighted sound pressure level L_{Aeq} (dBA)
Within 32 ft/10 m three-lane roadway (e.g., highway 60–70 mph/95–110 kph)	70–90
Within 32 ft/10 m of a main urban road (30–40 mph/45–65 kph)	65–75
Suburban area screened from main road by intervening buildings	55–65
Parkland within a large town or city	55–60
Secluded country location	35–45

to provide a buffer between a major existing source such as a road and any residential buildings can be beneficial.

- Situate private amenity space (e.g., backyard/gardens) away from significant noise, e.g., a road/railway. The dwelling can be used to protect a back yard/garden.

- Use communal space, parking, landscaping areas that are already allowed for in the development as buffer zones to increase the standoff distance between noise-sensitive buildings and a noise source (road, railway, etc.).

- Figure 4.1 shows the use of either commercial buildings (strip mall) or flats/apartments to provide a barrier block to houses that could be affected by road noise. When the barrier block is flats/apartments, it

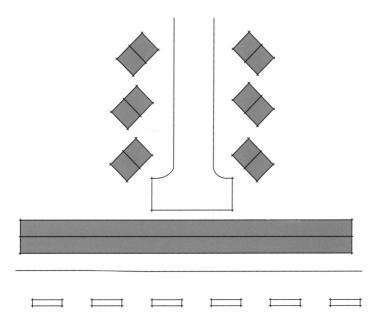

4.1 Barrier block (residential or commercial) used to protect dwellings from noise source (in this instance, a road)

is possible to allow for higher noise levels outside the building, as it is anticipated that there would be no private amenity space on this façade.

■ When providing balcony or roof terrace space for flats/apartments, try to locate them so they do not have a clear line of site to any significant noise source.

4.2.3 Controlling noise through distance

The use of distance as a means of controlling noise can be effective but only if the size of a site allows for substantial standoff distances. The greater the distance a building is from a noise source then the quieter the level of noise from the source will be within the building. This will depend upon whether the noise source is considered as a *point source*, such as HVAC equipment, or a *line source*, such as noise from a railway line or highway. If a house were located 65 ft (20 m) from a railway line or a road, this would be considered a line source and so the level of noise would be reduced by 13 dB relative to the measured noise level at the source. If the house were 65 ft (20 m) from a point source (a lawnmower or AC unit), the level would be reduced by 26 dB.

As a general rule of thumb, the difference between line source and point source attenuation is:

■ –3 dB reduction in noise level for each doubling of distance from a line source (road/rail)
■ –6 dB reduction in noise level for each doubling of distance from a point source (fixed plant/HVAC).

The following rules of thumb can be applied when considering the development of a site within an urban environment:

■ Any development site which is more than 328 ft (100 m) from a major road is unlikely to need control measures for road traffic noise.
■ Any development site which is more than 985 ft (300 m) from a major large-scale industrial complex is unlikely to need control measures for industrial noise.
■ Any development site which is more than 820 ft (250 m) from a main rail route (heavy freight and/or high-speed passenger) is unlikely to need control measures for rail traffic noise.

For aircraft noise, suitable distances will not only be dependent upon the existing noise environment but also on the number of runways, volume of aircraft movement, and whether or not the development site is under the flight path or parallel to the flight path. For reference, noise levels for an Airbus 320A can be as high as 85 dB at a distance of 985 ft (300 m) during takeoff.

Eqs. A.5 and A.6 outline suitable methods for calculating distance attenuation.

4.2.4 Controlling noise with barriers

By including barriers in site designs, it is possible to reduce overall noise levels further. The idea of using a building as a barrier is one possible method, but the most common method would be to construct a fence, bund, or berm.

By breaking the direct line of sight between a noise source and the receiver (a person or a building), we reduce the level of sound because we are increasing the distance the sound has to travel between source and receiver (i.e., the sound has to go over the top of the barrier). A good rule of thumb is to ensure that the barrier is at least 2 ft (0.6 m) above the receiver's head height (Figure 4.2).

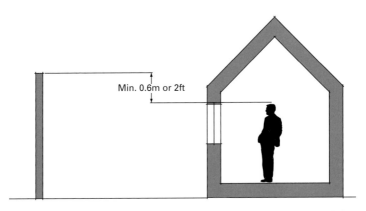

Min. 0.6m or 2ft

4.2 Minimum height barrier should extend over receiver height to ensure line of sight is broken (assuming comparable ground level between source and site)

Figure 4.3 shows some common barrier arrangements. Barriers work best if they are placed either close to the noise source or close to the noise receiver, rather than centered between both.

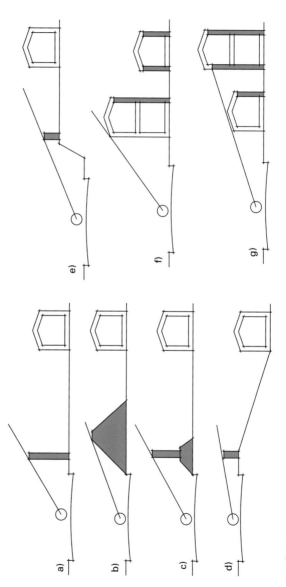

4.3 Barrier arrangements

The circles in Figure 4.3 represent the noise source, with the line of sight possible shown by the straight lines:

a) A simple barrier that can be constructed from close-boarded timber or a proprietary barrier system.

b) A bund or berm formed from earth. Flat-topped berms tend to provide greater levels of reduction, but the required land can be substantial.

c) A combined bund and barrier. Useful in providing sufficient height, but reducing the land requirement.

d) Dropping the site level below that of the noise source can mean that the required barrier height is reduced. *Note*: If the barrier is placed next to the noise receiver, it would have to be significantly higher to break the line of sight.

e) Increasing the site level can also reduce the required barrier height. *Note*: If the noise source is in a cutting, a canyon effect can occur where the noise is bounced off the sides of the cutting and can negate the beneficial effects of site level difference.

f) The tall building provides screening to the back and the smaller building behind.

g) Placing a smaller building in front can, however, be just as effective, as a greater area of the total façades can be protected. The additional distance and the partial screening to the upper front façade of the rear building contribute to the overall reduction of noise. A similar effect can be achieved with podium design buildings.

The level of attenuation for an acoustic barrier will depend on the following factors.

- The height of the barrier: the higher the barrier, the greater its expected performance.
- The type of noise source: barriers are more effective for stationary noise sources such as HVAC or a road than for a moving source such as tractor that roams around a field.
- The height of the noise source: the higher the source, the higher the barrier will have to be to break the line of site.
- The height of the receiver: the higher the receiver is, the higher the barrier will have to be to break the line of site.

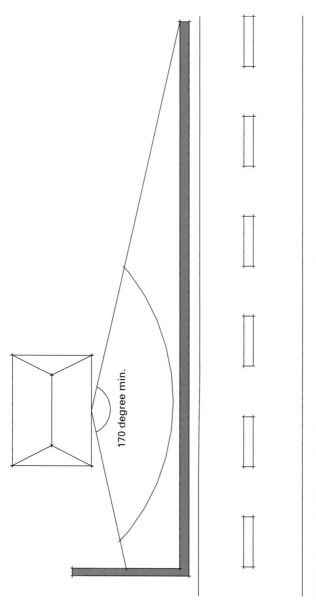

170 degree min.

4.4 Using barriers to break horizontal line of sight either by a long barrier or a wraparound barrier

Table 4.3 Basic sound reduction levels from acoustic barriers

Type of barrier	Noise level reduction
Full barrier (full break in line of sight from source to receiver)	10 dB
Partial barrier (partial break in line of sight from source to receiver)	5 dB

- The mass of the barrier: generally the minimum surface mass of any acoustic barrier should not be less than 22 lb/ft^2 (10 kg/m^2).
- The barrier must provide a minimum of 170-degree control of view from the receiver position to the source. This can often be more easily achieved by doglegging or bending a barrier around the receiver (see Figure 4.4).
- Openings and gaps in a barrier should be avoided. Total openings, gaps, or cracks should not exceed 1 percent of the surface area (total openings of as little as 4 percent would result in a performance as low as 4 dB).
- Double barriers are often not very effective, as the bulk of any attenuation will be due to the highest barrier.

The calculation of the attenuation offered by an acoustic barrier can be complicated. One possible calculation method is shown in Figure A.1, Eq. A.7. Table 4.3 outlines a good rule of thumb for basic barrier design.

For example, a 6 ft (2 m) barrier is likely to provide 10 dB reduction from road traffic at ground-floor level and 5 dB reduction at first-floor level.

4.2.5 Trees and vegetation

A common misconception is that the use of a strip of trees or shrubs can be used as an effective means of controlling noise. While living noise barriers (solid barriers created from earth and vegetation) can be extremely effective, naturally spread trees and shrubs are not. This is not to say that they cannot be beneficial. By providing a visual screen, they can help to reduce the perception of noise as an issue, particularly if the sound source is mobile. They can also help to provide some masking noise as a result of wind blowing through leaves and branches. When considering these benefits, keep in mind the seasonal variations of the type of vegetation you choose.

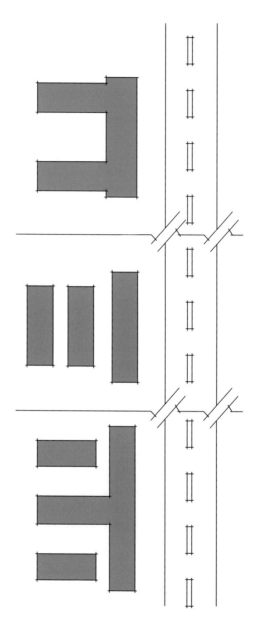

4.5 Optimum large building layouts to protect façades from noise, e.g., where road noise is the source (adapted from BRE/CIRIA, 1993)

4.2.6 Optimum building shapes to control external noise

The aim should be to ensure that the maximum number of rooms are screened from a noise source and the positioning of any building does not result in noise reflecting from one façade to another. Figure 4.5 shows the most advantageous layouts for controlling noise to a large area of façade for large-scale developments (e.g., schools, hospitals).

4.2.7 Angle of view to control external noise

The orientation of a building or a noise sensitive room away from a noise source can also reduce the level of noise disturbance. Where a room directly overlooks a noise source (road, railway line, etc.) the design is entirely dependent upon the distance from the source or the inclusion of an acoustic barrier for attenuation. If the room is angled away from the source then there is an expected reduction in noise due to the angle of view between the receiver and the source. Table 4.4 outlines the expected reductions in sound levels at 500 Hz and 1000 Hz dependent on the angle of view from source to receiver.

Table 4.4 Angle of view correction

Building orientation		Sound attenuation (dB)	
		500Hz	1000Hz
0°		0	0
45°		1	1
90°		6	6
135°		15	17
180°		17	19

4.2.8 Balconies and parapets

The use of balconies and terraces with solid barriers or parapets can be an effective means of reducing noise getting to the building façade. However, it should always be noted that by providing balconies and terraces we create outdoor amenity space that may be exposed to significant levels of noise (see Figure 4.6). Another technique that has been adopted has been to install a false glazed façade detail set out from the front of the actual façade, to provide a translucent screen in front of the windows.

1   Solid parapet wall to front of balcony can help to reduce line of sight between the rooms and an external noise source.
2   Setting overhangs above the façade line can help to further reduce the angle of view to an external noise source, and provides an exposed external soffit that can be lined with an absorptive material to help further reduce noise levels around the balcony/terrace.

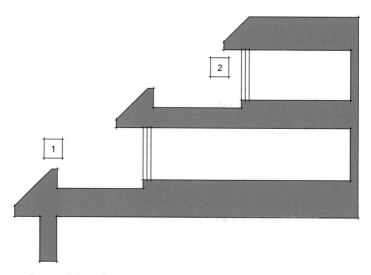

4.6 Protective balconies/terraces

4.2.9 Fin walls and angled glazing

The use of fin walls along balcony or roof terrace areas can help to screen the windows or doors that look out onto these areas. This, along with a reduced angle of view, can help limit overall noise levels within the buildings. Similarly, where the building cannot be oriented away from the source, the location of any glazing can be chosen so that it does not face onto the noise source, or the window can even be oriented so that it does not have the same angle of view as the wall itself (see Figure 4.7).

4.2.10 Single-aspect buildings

It can be difficult to achieve suitable internal levels, due to the noise exposure experienced on a particular façade. In such instances, the design of single-aspect buildings can be adopted. This is most often a factor in the design of dwellings and means that noise-sensitive rooms such as living rooms and bedrooms are located to the quiet side of a building, while non-sensitive areas such as corridors, bathrooms, and kitchens can be located on the noisy side of a building. Figures 4.8 and 4.9 provide suggested floor plans for a three-story town house and for a two-bedroom flat/apartment where it is necessary to keep noise-sensitive rooms away from the rear façade (e.g., bedrooms and living rooms).

4.2.11 Glazing

The primary method for reducing noise within a building from external sources is through the specification of the building envelope. As external façades are usually composite constructions (wall, glass, and ventilation), it is possible to determine the total attenuation of the system through composite façade calculations (see Eq. A.17). However, it is generally the case that the weakest element in the façade will dictate the overall level of insulation. Allowing for attenuated ventilation usually means that the specification of suitable glazing will dictate acoustic performance. With external walls likely to provide significantly higher levels of acoustic insulation by concentrating on glazing specifications, we can take a cautious approach to façade design and ensure that internal requirements are achieved.

It is commonly accepted that, for some noise sources (commercial noise and industrial noise), internal noise levels within an affected building should be determined in relation to an open window. In many other instances (transportation noise in particular), the assessment of internal noise levels

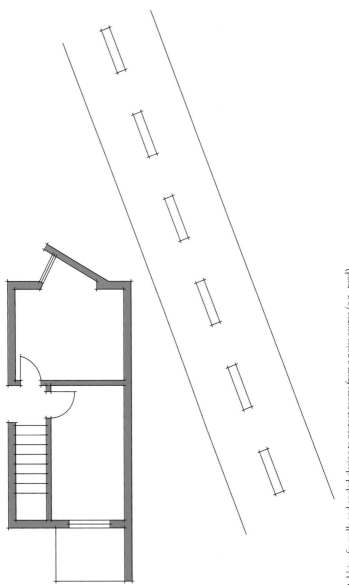

4.7 Using fin walls and angled glazing to protect rooms from a noise source (e.g., road)

GROUND FLOOR   FIRST FLOOR   SECOND FLOOR

4.8 Three-story house where noise-sensitive rooms are on one façade

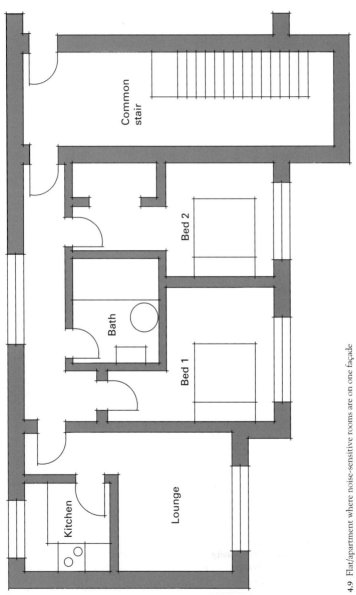

4.9 Flat/apartment where noise-sensitive rooms are on one façade

can be determined with closed windows. A wide range of acoustic performance data is published by most glazing manufacturers and will normally
detail frequency performance levels along with average or single-figure values.

When selecting a glazing unit, it is best to base any assessment on a
performance parameter which rates the window against a low frequency noise
source (e.g., R_{TRA} or $R'_w + C_{tr}$). This is the reduction (R) in noise level provided by the glazing unit when adjusted for a traffic noise spectrum (TRA).
Table 4.5 details the expected insulation values for some typical glazing specifications. In addition, it shows expected levels of reduction (D_w) from open
windows depending on the source of noise.

As the majority of data provided with regards to glazing performance
is based on laboratory testing, it is necessary to consider frame design. The
following good practice should be adopted:

■ Solid window frames (e.g., timber) tend to provide higher levels of
   performance over hollow frame systems (e.g., aluminum or uPVC).

Table 4.5 Insulation values for open and closed glazing units (higher values equate
to higher levels of insulation) (Waters-Fuller 2005)

Open windows – expected D_w for windows with a free open area of 0.05 m²	D_w dBA
Road traffic noise	12–18
Railway noise	12–18
Aircraft noise	14–19
Amplified music	15–20

Closed windows – expected RTRA dB insulation values for typical glazing types	
Glazing type	RTRA dB
4 mm float glass / 12 mm cavity / 4 mm float glass	25
6 mm float glass / 12 mm cavity / 6 mm float glass	26
6 mm float glass / 12 mm cavity / 6.4 laminate glass	27
10 mm float glass / 12 mm cavity / 4 mm float glass	29
6 mm float glass / 12 cavity / 7 float glass	31
10 mm float glass / 12 mm cavity / 6 mm float glass	32
6 mm float glass / 12 cavity / 11 mm float glass	33
10 mm float glass / 12 cavity / 6.4 mm laminate glass	34

■ The acoustic performance of hollow window frames can be significantly improved with fiber or foam within the frame cavities, or with composite cladding to the frame (e.g., aluminum frames with timber facings).

■ Gaps between the window frame and the façade should be packed and sealed prior to fitting of internal and external facings. Gaps which are greater than 25 mm (1 in) should first be packed with a mineral fiber material, then sealed front and back with a flexible sealant.

4.2.12 Roof design

The acoustic design of any roof structure should aim to ensure control from both airborne noise and rain noise.

As a general rule, tile or shingle pitched roofs which have loft space and are insulated using a fibrous material are likely to provide sufficiently high levels of acoustic insulation, so noise from external sources and rain noise are unlikely to be an issue. The only exception to this would be for dwellings which are to be located under an airport flight path.

Similarly, heavy concrete roof structures, ballasted roofs, and green roof systems where vegetation is placed on the roof are expected to provide adequate levels of acoustic control from airborne noise and rain noise for most building types and situations.

While lightweight metal roofs can be perceived as being problematic, it is possible to ensure noise is sufficiently controlled through good design. The following should be considered when selecting a roofing system:

■ Multi-layer synthetic roofing membranes (minimum 3/32 in/2 mm) and bituminous roofing membranes can provide good levels of rain noise control even when used on rigid insulation panels. Insulation of the roof structure will be further improved by plasterboard or mineral fiber tile ceiling systems.

■ When steel or aluminum roofing systems are detailed, the use of a damp-ening membrane to the underside of the roofing panel (minimum 3/32 in/2 mm) is recommended to help reduce rain noise.

■ Steel or aluminum built-up roofing systems which use mineral fiber insulation materials tend to provide inherently better levels of acoustic control than pre-fabricated composite roof panels which use rigid insulation materials.

■ Pre-fabricated composite roofing panels which use rigid insulation can be significantly enhanced with the introduction of a fibrous absorption layer and/or a mass layer to the overall roof systems (e.g., high-density mineral fiber quilt or plasterboard ceilings).

Table 4.6 provides details of some typical roof structures and their expected acoustic performance.

Alterations to ceiling systems can also enhance acoustic performance, for example upgrading from standard ceiling tiles to plasterboard backed tiles can increase insulation levels up to 4–6 dB.

Table 4.6 Insulation values for typical roof constructions

Specification	STC/R_w (dB)
Traditional roof structure – Tile/slate or shingle on 50 mm battens, 12 mm plywood or timber boards/secondary layer, 160 mm timber rafters fully filled with mineral fiber insulation, vapor check layer, 30 mm timber battens, x1 layer 15 mm plasterboard	53–55
Concrete roof structure, suspended tile ceiling – Waterproof layer with or without ballast covering over insulation board, 100 mm (nominal) cast in-situ slab, suspended metal frame, min 100 mm cavity lined with mineral fiber ceiling tiles	52–55
Concrete roof structure, plasterboard ceiling – Waterproof layer with or without ballast covering over insulation board, 100 mm (nominal) cast in-situ slab, suspended metal frame, min 100 mm cavity lined with x1 layer 12.5 mm plasterboard	55–57
Flat timber roof with bituminous lining – Bituminous/asphalt roofing membrane, 12–15 mm ply or timber boarding, 100–120 mm timber roof joists fully filled with mineral fiber insulation, vapor check layer, x1 layer 12.5 mm plasterboard	43–46
Built-up flat roof system – Metal outer liner (e.g., standing seam roof) on top hat section, mineral fiber insulation layer nominal 200 mm, vapor control layer, 50 mm mineral fiber insulation, profiled steel or aluminum sheet	33–36
Built-up flat roof system with plasterboard ceiling – Metal outer liner (e.g. standing seam roof) on top hat section, mineral fiber insulation layer nominal 200 mm, vapor control layer, 50 mm mineral fiber insulation, profiled steel or aluminum sheet. Metal frame suspended grid system, minimum cavity 150 mm with 12.5 mm plasterboard	44–46

Table 4.6 **continued**

Specification	STC/R_w (dB)
Built-up flat roof system with suspended tile ceiling – Metal outer liner (e.g. standing seam roof) on top hat section, mineral fiber insulation layer nominal 200 mm, vapor control layer, 50 mm mineral fiber insulation, profiled steel or aluminum sheet. Metal frame suspended grid system, minimum cavity 150 mm with mineral fiber ceiling tile	41–43
Pre-fabricated flat roofing panel – 45 mm PU insulated roofing panel on top hat section, 60 mm high-density mineral fiber insulation material within cavity formed by top hat section, 0.7 mm steel liner tray on purlins	43–46
Pre-fabricated flat roofing system with plasterboard ceiling – 45 mm PU insulated roofing panel on top hat section, 60 mm high-density mineral fiber insulation material within cavity formed by top hat section, 0.7 mm steel liner tray on purlins. Metal frame suspended grid system, minimum cavity 150 mm with 12.5 mm plasterboard.	54–58
Pre-fabricated flat roofing system with suspended tile ceiling – 45 mm PU insulated roofing panel on top hat section, 60 mm high-density mineral fiber insulation material within cavity formed by top hat section, 0.7 mm steel liner tray on purlins. Metal frame suspended grid system, minimum cavity 150 mm with suspended tile ceiling	51–54

4.3 Internal mechanical noise control

MECHANICAL SYSTEMS ARE EVER-PRESENT in buildings today in most climates. Human comfort temperatures have been defined slightly differently in different countries; however, most users will adjust their building temperature mechanically if the temperatures are below 50°F or above 100°F (10°C or 38°C respectively). There are a few mechanical systems that are quiet by nature – for example, radiant systems that work by natural convection rather than using fans to promote air circulation – but most mechanical systems produce some degree of noise.

The noisy parts of a mechanical system unit are basically the compressor and the fan. By looking at where these parts are located, mechanical systems can be divided in three categories according to their noise-producing ability.

4.3.1 Fan and compressor in the room

Packaged units or window air-conditioning units have all parts in one enclosure, which is inside the space they are meant to heat/refrigerate. This means that, if you want to adjust your temperature, you need to tolerate the resulting noise. They can vary in noise levels depending on age and fabrication, but there is no such thing as a "quiet" compressor. This type of mechanical system is not recommended for any space where the acoustical environment is important.

4.3.2 Fan in room

Commonly called split systems, they have half of the parts outside the room (the compressor side) and half inside the room (the fan side). The noise is only produced by the fan, and the compressor part is completely separated from the room (outside the building rather than in a mechanical closet with ventilation grills towards the room). This type of equipment can be used in spaces that have somewhat low noise requirements, but not very high acoustical requirements, such as a concert hall or theater, where very low noise levels are sought.

4.3.3 Fan and compressor remote

Central systems are those where all parts of the mechanical equipment are located remotely from the room they intend to heat/refrigerate. The mechanical room is connected to the room by ducts that bring the already-temperature-controlled air. Several conditions should be considered when designing this type of system, to avoid noise traveling through the ducts (Figure 4.10).

1 Allow for use of acoustic louvers for ventilation apertures.
2 Allow additional space around unit for incorporation of acoustic enclosure.
3 Line ceilings with robust absorbent materials to help reducing overall noise levels within mechanical rooms.
4 Isolation of equipment should be allowed for. Isolation efficiencies of 95 percent should be seen as a suitable standard.

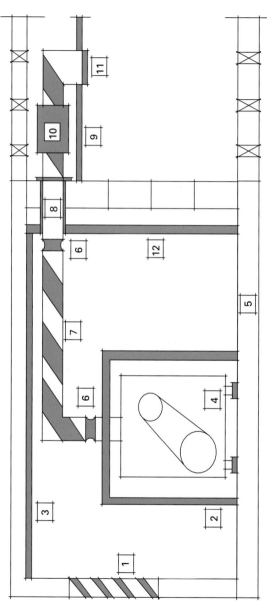

4.10 Central system (remote fan/compressor) mechanical room layout

5   Machine-room floors should be high mass, such as concrete. Concrete ceiling structures are also advisable.

6   Flexible connectors which isolate duct noise are recommended where a duct connects with a machine, and also just prior to where a duct penetrates through a wall.

7   Lagging of ductwork is recommended (see "Central system checklist" below).

8   Ducts should be lined with a closed cell foam or fibrous sleeve where they penetrate though a wall, to reduce contact with the wall structure. Any gaps at the duct exit should allow for a cover plate (e.g., plasterboard) cut round the duct to seal any gaps.

9   A plasterboard or acoustically insulating ceiling tile should be specified where noise from the duct is anticipated and room noise sensitivity is high.

10 For noise-sensitive rooms, silencers or attenuators may be required prior to the duct termination point.

11 Acoustic grills can be fitted to duct outlets.

Rooftop units Even though rooftop units are technically part of the central system category, they have different acoustic issues of their own. The fact that they could be located right above a space intended to be quiet defeats the purpose. Unwanted vibrations can produce additional noise in the rooms below, and the ceiling partition is the only barrier between the noise source and the room. This type of system is often the culprit for community disputes, due to the fact that the equipment could be well isolated from the building it serves but in direct line of sight with a neighboring building.

Central system checklist

■   Ducts distributing air to several spaces should branch out instead of connecting them directly.

■   Turbulence noise in turns can be avoided by circular elbows, turning vanes, and silencers.

■   Lining inside the duct is more efficient acoustically but can bring poor air-quality conditions. Lining outside ducts is less efficient, but keeps glass fibers far from the air stream. Double duct systems allow for acoustic lining between two walls of the duct.

■   Rooftop units should not be located above noise-sensitive spaces. They need to be properly isolated from the structure to avoid vibration transferring to the building, and they need to be properly isolated from other buildings nearby.

■ Diffusers and grills that connect the duct to the space will produce more noise at higher air speeds and when halfway closed will reduce air flow.

Further reading

British Standards Institution (BSI) (1997) *Method for rating industrial noise affecting mixed residential and industrial areas*. BS4142:1997. London: BSI.

British Standards Institution (BSI) (2009) *Noise and vibration control on construction and open sites – Part 1. Code of practice for basic information and procedures for noise and vibration control*. BS5228-1:2009. London: BSI.

British Standards Institution (BSI) (1999) *Sound insulation and noise reduction for buildings, code of practice*. BS8233:1999. London: BSI.

Building Research Establishment & Construction Industry Research and Information Association (BRE/CIRIA) (1993) *Sound control for homes*. BR238/CIRIA Report 127. London: Crown Copyright.

Jaramillo, A. M., and Ermann, M. G. (2013) The link between HCAV type and student achievement. Unpublished doctoral dissertation, Virginia Polytechnic Institute and State University, Blacksburg, VA.

Mackenzie, R., et al. (2003) *A review of acoustic fencing*. Edinburgh: Edinburgh Napier University.

Waters-Fuller, T. (2005) *The development and production of a guide for noise control from laminate and wooden flooring*. London: Defra.

chapter 5

Room acoustics

WHEN STUDYING THE ACOUSTICS OF A BUILDING, we need to deal with all the phenomena mentioned in Chapter 2. In an enclosed space, sound waves will be modified by the interaction with the building elements.

5.1 Geometrical acoustics

5.1.1 Reflected sound and path differences

The use of absorptive materials is concerned with controlling reflected sound within a room. One of the purposes of controlling reflected sound with absorptive materials is to reduce the level of sound that arrives late enough after the direct sound, as this can cause disturbance and reduce speech intelligibility. By absorbing this sound, we reduce its energy and so reduce how far it can propagate or how loud it is perceived.

There are also instances where we want to encourage sound to be reflected off room surfaces, because if it arrives soon enough after the direct sound it can have the perceived effect of making a voice sound louder or clearer. Achieving these effects is dependent on the difference in time and on the difference in distance a sound wave has to travel. If we place a hard reflective surface close to a sound source and we know its position, its size, and the angle at which it is oriented, we can control the direction in which sound coming into contact with the panel will travel.

Figure 5.1 shows sound propagation out from a single source: Figure 5.1a shows the direct sound between source and listener along with the indirect sound being reflected off untreated surfaces allowing for long reverberation times as a result of the difference in paths. Figure 5.1b is after treatment with absorptive materials, to reduce the effects of late reflections of sound, and an acoustic reflector has also been added above the sound source.

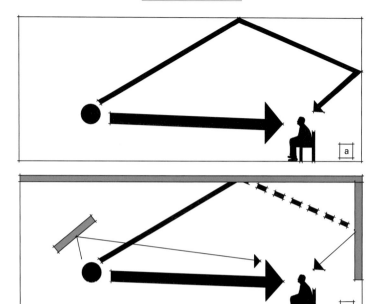

5.1 Absorbing and reflecting sound-path differences

The angle size and positioning of this panel encourages sound to be reflected, so that it arrives at the listener at the right time to help reinforce the sound level.

By understanding the position, size, and orientation of such reflective panels and the distribution of absorptive panels, we can design for better acoustics.

5.1.2 Optimum path differences

The path difference is linked to the difference in the time it takes for the direct sound to reach the listener, compared to the time taken for the indirect sound to reach the listener. Table 5.1 details optimum path differences and its effect on the listening environment.

As path differences between direct and reverberant sound are a result of sound waves being reflected off room surfaces, it is clear that the size, as well as the shape, of a room has a direct effect on acoustics. Get the room

Table 5.1 Subjective effect from differences in path lengths

Time delay (milliseconds)	Path difference		Condition
	Metric (m)	Imperial (feet/inches)	
<1	<0.3m	11"	Can cause disruption to the sound source
<20	0.3–7m	11"–22'11"	Excellent range for speech
20–30	7–10m	22'11"–32'9"	Good for speech
30–45	10–15m	32'9"–49'2"	Marginal
50–80	15–27m	49'2"–88'6"	Unsatisfactory

dimensions wrong, or place a reflective surface in the wrong position, and the acoustics will be poor.

5.1.3 Determining path difference

The mathematics used to predict path differences is detailed in Eq. A.8. For acoustically reflective panels, whether they are suspended or are taken to be the rear wall of an assembly room stage, the key property is the panel size. As long as the panel is between two and four times the size of the sound wave enacting upon it, then the angle of the sound wave going into the panel will be equal to the sound wave reflecting off the panel (Figure 2.2).

The most relevant frequencies to speech intelligibility lie between 1000 Hz and 4000 Hz, while the frequencies where the voice carries the greatest energy center around 500 Hz. Therefore the optimum size of reflective panels, for speech, would be between 4.25 ft^2 and 9 ft^2 (1.4 m^2 and 2.8 m^2).

5.2 Reverberation

IF YOU STAND IN A LARGE ROOM and make a sudden noise, you might hear an echo. The sound you first hear is the sound which has traveled directly from where the noise was created to your ear. The next time you hear the sound you have made is when it has traveled from you to one of the surfaces in the room and bounced back to where you are standing. As this sound has had to travel further, the time it takes for the sound to reach your ear is longer and differences in the timing are perceived as an echo. But, as we mentioned in Chapter 3, our brains have the ability to merge all reflections of sound that arrive at our ears during the first 50 ms, so early reflections won't be perceived as a distinct echo. Late reflections might not be perceived as echoes if they are not very loud. Instead, we perceive them as a permanence of sound that slowly decays. This is known in acoustics as reverberation.

5.2.1 The importance of reverberation within buildings

If the time delay between the direct sound and the reverberant sound is too long, it can adversely affect how well we hear speech or music, but if we can control and enhance the sounds which arrive soon after the direct sound, the early reflections, this can have the effect of improving sound quality.

Reverberation is present in all rooms of any size and shape. By knowing the shape, size, and materials that are used to create a room, we can define how reverberant that space will be, and so we can design avoiding the sort of problems associated with reverberation. It is often thought that the consideration of room acoustics is something which is limited to the design of music venues; however, if we do not consider reverberation when designing other buildings, then we run the risk of providing educational buildings where teaching becomes difficult, healthcare buildings where patient recovery is hampered, workspaces where people are easily distracted, and commercial spaces which customers do not feel comfortable using.

Through designing the reverberation of a room, we can:

■ alter the overall noise level within a space
■ make a space more or less suitable for a range of activities from quiet study to live music
■ create environments in which listening and understanding are enhanced.

5.2.2 Reverberation time

The phenomenon of reverberation is quantified by reverberation time (RT). It is defined as the time it takes a sound to decay 60 dB after the source has stopped emitting it. Reverberation times are given in seconds and they can be measured, calculated, or simulated. When measuring reverberation times in a room, it is not always possible to obtain a 60 dB decay. This means that, however high the noise floor (background noise) in the room is, the initial level of the sound before it starts decaying needs to be 60 dB above that (Figure 5.2a). For this reason, the measurement of reverberation time is usually extrapolated. In Figure 5.2b, we see that a 30 dB decay is measured from –5 dB to –35 dB below the starting level. If we then multiply this time by 2, it would be the same as measuring the entire 60 dB projected decay (T60). This is referred to as T30 and is equivalent to the calculated RT. T20 and T10

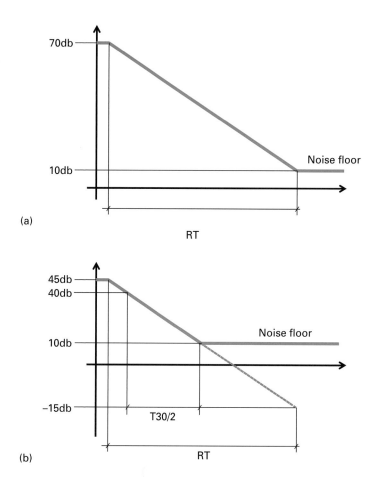

5.2 Reverberation time

are also commonly used, always subtracting 5 dB from the initial level to start counting down the desired decay.

5.2.3 How we control reverberation

We know that reverberation is caused when sound waves are reflected off a surface and back towards the source or towards a listener. By stopping some, most, or all of that sound from being reflected, we reduce the energy of the returning sound wave. This reduces the overall level of sound that is then heard. As a result, the reverberant sound is either eliminated or reduced to a level at which it is no longer perceived to cause a problem.

To stop sound being reflected, we use materials which are acoustically absorptive (see Section 2.5). They are generally softer material finishes or slim panel systems which may also have perforations or slots in them.

There are also instances where we may want to increase or maintain reverberation. By placing acoustically reflective materials closely behind a sound source, we can produce an effect that reinforces the sound being made. This is because we create an echo, which has a very short time interval between it and the first sound wave. Its close arrival has the effect of amplifying the sound.

Acoustically reflective materials will commonly be heavy and have hard, smooth, even surfaces.

5.2.4 Measuring reverberation

When acousticians measure the reverberation within a room, they will create a sudden impulsive or interruptive sound, often from a starter pistol or a loudspeaker. They will then use a microphone connected to a recording system, such as a sound-level meter, which will measure how long it takes the total noise level within the room to drop by a defined amount, e.g., 30 dB or 60 dB. As time progresses, the noise level reduces at each frequency. Reverberation times can vary from between a few seconds, common in large churches or cathedrals, to a few fractions of a second, common in bedrooms or living rooms. The shorter the time it takes for the sound to reduce, the less reverberant a space is and so the greater the quantity of absorptive finishes. Longer reverberation times usually mean less absorptive materials in a room as well as a larger volume of space being enclosed.

Over the last 100 years, assessments of reverberation times in common spaces have been undertaken to determine the optimum level or reverberation.

The optimum reverberation time will be dependent upon the room size and what the room is to be used for, such as speech or music. From these assessments it has been possible to derive good practice guidelines of reverberation times in common spaces.

Appendix B provides more detailed recommendations for specific room types, while Appendix A, Eq. A.25 provides a calculation method that can be used to determine the optimum reverberation time, dependent on room size and whether it is to be used for speech, music or choral music.

5.2.5 Predicting reverberation

The beneficial aspect of having optimum reverberation times is that not only can they be accurately measured in completed buildings, but it is also possible to predict reverberation times with a good degree of accuracy. This means that we can design rooms so that they are suitable for their intended use.

For acousticians, the Sabine equation or the Norris-Eyring equation are familiar design tools used in calculating reverberation times; however, they may be less familiar to architects and designers. An explanation of these two calculations is given in Appendix A (see Eq. A.22 and A.23). For the purposes of basic design, the key elements to be aware of are room volume, the materials chosen as surface finishes, room shape, and the angle of room surfaces.

Taking an atrium space as an example, here we have a space which is likely to be large – therefore reverberation, particularly at lower frequencies, is likely to be high; there will be long reverberation times due to the time it takes for a sound wave to reach a boundary surface and be returned. In addition, atrium spaces are likely to have a lot of glass and even hard floor surfaces. These hard surfaces are efficient at reflecting sound and as a result the sound wave being returned does not lose a lot of energy.

Contrast an atrium with a small bedroom. The distance the sound has to travel from the source until it reaches a boundary surface is small; therefore reverberation times are short. In addition, bedrooms are likely to have carpeted floors, curtains, as well as the soft materials associated with a bed mattress and bedding. These materials are poor at reflecting sound, because they tend to absorb a lot of the energy of the sound wave. As a result there is less sound returned to the listener.

If we want to change the acoustics of an atrium or a bedroom, it is unlikely that we will have the option of reducing or increasing the volume of the space, so we tend to rely on techniques which impact on the strength of a reverberant sound wave, usually through altering absorption or directing the sound waves where we want them to go. It is here the architect or designer has a part to play, as these control methods can have a visual impact on a finished space.

5.2.6 Distribution of sound absorption in a room

For common room types, the general rule to follow is that acoustically absorptive materials should be spread evenly around the space. This is because it is assumed that no single position would be considered to be the primary source position for speech or music. The aim is to ensure equal control of noise buildup and speech intelligibility at any position within the space.

Figure 5.3 details some common methods of distribution for absorptive materials.

5.2.7 Room shape and its influence on acoustics

The ideal shape of a room for good acoustics varies with the room function, the capacity requirements, and architectural constraints. As a result it is a complex issue that demands greater depth than can be allowed for in this book. While shoebox-shaped rooms have been found to be good for orchestral music, particular classical choral music may favor a more churchlike space. Whether the development of these styles influenced building design, or the shape of the building influenced the style of the music, is a subject of debate, but what is clear is that some shapes do cause potential acoustic problems that should be known to the designer.

Narrow corridors can result in echoes becoming an issue, as sound is reflected off of two parallel walls. This can be a particular problem in hotels. Good levels of absorptive finishes, plaster or timber moldings on wall surfaces, and fire doors across corridors can help to reduce this effect.

Curved ceiling or curved alcoves and walls can allow for sound to be focused on a particular position, causing issues with sound clarity, particularly in theater or music venues. In addition, echoes are also possible along the curve of large domes (often creating whispering galleries where sound is reflected along a ceiling to the opposite side of a room). The addition of acoustically absorbent linings or suspended acoustic reflector panels can help to reduce focusing. The application of these and plaster or timber moldings, or less reflective wall finishes, can significantly reduce the effect of whispering galleries.

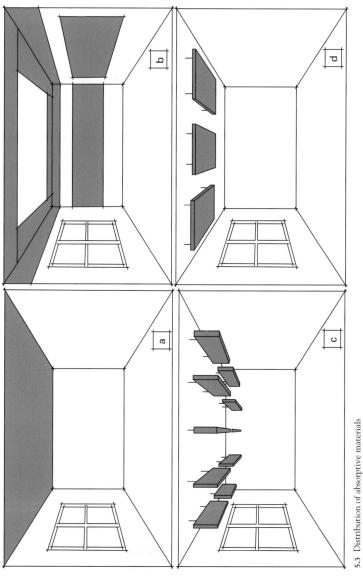

5.3 Distribution of absorptive materials

Parallel walls in music rooms should be avoided. Walls should be offset by a minimum of 5 degrees to avoid the potential for standing waves to occur (areas of high or low sound pressure). This can be achieved by building rooms that are not perfectly square or rectangular, or by applying angled surfaces after completion of the structural room elements (see Figure 5.3).

a) Most commonly achieved with a mineral fiber ceiling system. Performance is dictated by the classification of the ceiling tile. Even tiles with a low NRC classification can be improved by placing a deep layer of mineral fiber quilt above the tile. As a large area is covered, performance at lower frequencies can be enhanced. If ceiling heights are particularly high, overall performance can be reduced, as there may be insufficient absorption at head height, e.g., games halls.

b) Most commonly achieved with wall- and ceiling-mounted acoustically absorptive panels. This method is preferable in buildings where concrete soffits may need to be exposed to capture thermal mass. The untreated area in the center of the ceiling can be beneficial for board rooms, as it allows reinforcing early reflections to reach multiple listening positions, but only where ceiling heights are kept low. Wall panels allow for the additional absorption lost on the ceiling and for some improvement at low frequencies.

c) Vertically suspended absorptive panels are also useful for designs where thermal mass is used. Thicker vertically suspended panels can be very efficient, as they have two sides which absorb sound. Similar alternatives would be suspended geometric shapes or architectural shapes, which can add visual interest. Vertically suspended tiles can be limited in performance at low frequencies due to the surface area of each panel.

d) Cloud or horizontally suspended panels can provide similar levels of absorption to whole ceiling treatments, although they may cause limiting factors if the use of thermal mass is a consideration. They can be specified in a variety of shapes to add visual interest. The height at which they are suspended can be altered to help reduce flutter echoes and also to create effective lower ceiling heights in areas where speech intelligibility or privacy are more important. Low frequency performance will be dictated by panel dimensions.

(see Figure 5.3, page 77)

5.3 Early Decay Time, EDT

A SIMILAR ACOUSTIC PARAMETER to reverberation time is the EDT. This is defined as six times the time it takes sound to decay by 10 dB after the source has stopped emitting. If you put the definitions of EDT and RT together, you'll realize that for a straight decay (single slope) they will be exactly the same. However, there are instances where a double slope decay exists and both values can greatly differ.

EDT has been commonly considered as having a closer relation to our perception of reverberation than reverberation time itself.

5.3.1 Double slope decay

Most rooms will have a single slope decay of sound. This means sound will decay at a steady rate until it's gone. But double sloped rooms are not uncommon. Basically this will occur when a room has two distinct spaces in it. These can be a stage house built as a distinct volume connected to the room by a proscenium wall, or the space under a very deep balcony which becomes a second distinct room. Even the space above a ceiling cloud can become a second space if the reflectors are very close to each other.

These are all examples of unintentional double slope rooms; however, it is possible to design a room to have a double slope by building another room around the venue that connects to it with apertures that can be varied. It can be the hallway that has access to the side balconies, or a room for no other purpose than creating a second reverberation time. In all these cases the listener in the main room will perceive the reverberation of that room, followed by the late arrival of another reverberation with a different rate of decay. In Figure 5.4, we have three cases:

a)   RT = EDT in a single slope room
b)   RT > EDT in a double slope room
c)   RT < EDT in a double slope room.

When we intentionally design a room to have a double slope, we are looking for case (b). The shorter EDT will give clarity to speech or music due to the short decay of sound, but the longer RT will increase enveloping of the listener by a low-level longer reverberation.

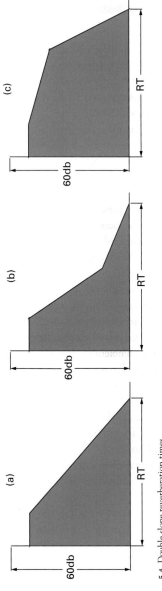

5.4 Double slope reverberation times

5.4 Signal to noise ratio, SNR

THE DIFFERENCE IN LEVEL between the main signal of interest and the background noise is called signal-to-noise ratio (SNR or S/N).

The relationship between the sound level of, say, a person's voice at the listener's position, and the overall ambient noise within a room (i.e., the noise from all other contributing sources) has an effect on how easy it is to understand what is being said. While we aim to provide acceptable ambient noise levels within unoccupied rooms, it is not uncommon for noise levels within occupied rooms to be significantly higher (e.g., ambient levels of around L_{Aeq} 55 dB are common in classrooms where all the students are working quietly). With natural speech levels of around L_{Aeq} 65 dB being usual in close proximity to the person's voice (within 3 ft/1 m), it does not take a great deal of separation between a person speaking and a listener for the voice to be drowned out by other noise sources. A person seated more than 10 ft (3 m) from a speaker has a very real risk of not being able to hear what is being said even in a relatively quiet environment.

The aim is to ensure that there is a large enough difference between the sound level of the speaker's voice and the ambient noise level within a space. We can control this either through reducing the distance between person speaking and listener, or by controlling noise buildup within the room through the control of background noise and reducing reverberation. Figure 5.5 details the permissible ambient noise levels in order to maintain either a 10 dB, 15 dB, or 20 dB signal to noise ratio (SNR) i.e., to ensure that the difference between the sound level from the person's voice and the overall noise level in the room is either 10 dB, 15 dB, or 20 dB.

If the listener is likely to be more than 16 ft (5 m) from a speaker, then it is necessary to control ambient noise levels at that position to below L_{Aeq} 40 dB when the room is in use. As a general rule of thumb we can subtract a further 5–10 dB to give us a reasonable margin for error; hence a target value of L_{Aeq} 30–35 dB would be suitable. Guidelines on suitable ambient noise levels within a range of buildings and specific levels for sound insulation, ambient noise control, acceptable mechanical noise levels, and maximum permissible reverberation times are detailed in Appendix B.

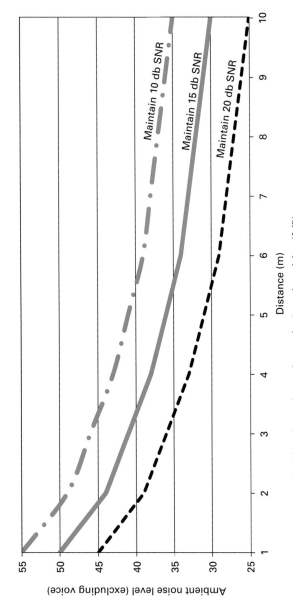

5.5 Permissible ambient noise levels dependent on distance from speaker (normal speech L_{Aeq} 65 dB)

5.5 Speech intelligibility

THE MOST IMPORTANT ACOUSTIC PARAMETER for spaces intended for speech is intelligibility. What good is a classroom or a church if words cannot be understood?

Speech intelligibility is affected by several characteristics of the room:

- Reverberation time: The longer the reverberation time, the lower the speech intelligibility.
- Distance between the source and receiver: The longer the distance, the lower the speech intelligibility.
- Background noise level: The higher the noise level, the lower the speech intelligibility.
- Signal to noise ratio: The smaller the difference between signal and background noise levels, the lower the speech intelligibility.

This means that, to obtain the desired levels of speech intelligibility, we need to consider moderate-size, very quiet, dead rooms. Of course, this is not always possible and we need to guarantee speech intelligibility under adverse circumstances. In order to increase the SNR, for example, we can place reflectors close to the source to act as amplifiers of sound. In order to reduce the noise levels we can place the listener the farthest away from the noise source.

5.5.1 % Articulation Loss of Consonants (% ALCons)

For many years, a common way to measure speech intelligibility required testing people in a room by reading long lists of meaningless short words and have them writing what they heard. The percentage of loss of consonants was then the percentage below 100 that speech intelligibility in the room was achieved.

5.5.2 Speech Transmission Index (STI)

In current years different ways to evaluate speech intelligibility have been created, especially to avoid the use of people in subjective tests. STI is not really a measurement of speech intelligibility, but a predictor of it. It takes into account the two acoustic parameters that most affect intelligibility: noise and reverberation. STI is a measure of the loss of modulation in a signal. This loss of modulation is attributed to sound reflections and background noise.

The following outlines performance for speech intelligibility (adapted from BS EN 60268-16, 2011). *Note*: A change of 0.1 in the STI is equal to a 3 dB change in the effective signal to noise ratio.

- ■ >0.76 = excellent intelligibility, but difficult to achieve (Class A+)
- ■ 0.66–0.74 = high speech intelligibility common in theaters (Class A–C)
- ■ 0.62–0.5 = good speech intelligibility common in offices and set as target ranges for public address systems (Class D–G)
- ■ 0.46–<0.36 = poor speech intelligibility, difficult environment for normal or amplified speech (Class H–U)

Further reading

British Standards Institution (BSI) (2011) *Sound system equipment – Part 16: Objective rating of speech intelligibility by speech transmission index*. BS EN 60268-16. London: BSI.

chapter 6

Sound measurements

AMPLITUDE IS THE CHARACTERISTIC of sound that we are usually inter-ested in measuring – "how loud" – and it can be measured as a whole or at a specific frequency or frequency band.

Human ears are very complex and don't have a flat response to sound either in frequency or sound pressure level. We have already talked about the use of decibels to explain sound pressure levels instead of the absolute units of sound pressure; we have also discussed the varying sensitivity of our ears in terms of frequency.

6.1 The decibel (dB)

IN CHAPTER 1 WE TALKED ABOUT sound amplitude being expressed in Pascals. This unit is not practical due to the enormous pressure range over which humans are able to sense sound. From the tiny pressure waves caused by the flapping of a bee's wings to the massive pressure waves created by the launch of Saturn 5 Rocket, it can be imagined how difficult it would be to plot these two pressure levels on a single graph (about seven orders of magnitude in pressure). At the same time, the perceptual response of human ears to sound amplitude is not linear but logarithmic. These are the reasons why the decibel scale was chosen to represent Sound Pressure Level (SPL or L_p). It is a comparison between the amplitude of a sound and that of the faintest audible sound for a human ear. The threshold of hearing is, of course, different for every single person but it was determined that, at 1 KHz, the average human threshold of hearing is about 2×10^{-5} Pa. The Sound Power can be derived from $L_p + 10 log S$ where S is the surface area of the sound wave (see Appendix A for more detail).

6.1.1 Human perception of loudness

As mentioned earlier, our ears do not respond to sound in a linear way. When we convert a sound pressure value to SPL in dB, we see that 3 dB are twice the sound pressure. However, 3 dB do not *sound* twice as loud to our ears. Instead, an increase of about 10 dB is necessary to produce a sound that we'd consider twice as loud; 5 dB, a noticeable difference; and 3 dB, only barely a noticeable difference.

6.2 Weighting curves

IN AN ATTEMPT TO CREATE a unit that could be used to measure sound, but at the same time represent what our ears are actually receiving (after all, why else do we want to measure sound if it isn't to see how it affects us?), the weighting curves were created. Figure 6.1 shows curves A, B, C, and D, used to weight sound pressure levels in decibels in order to better represent human hearing.

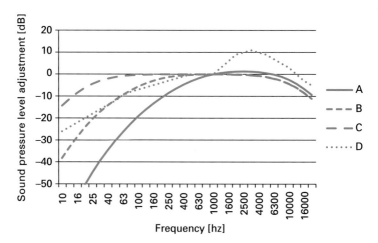

6.1 Weighting curves

6.2.1 A-weighting

The lowest curve was created to weight sounds at about 40 phons; however, this curve has been widely spread to the point where it is used nowadays to weight any sound. Environmental noise standards and noise ordinances use it instead of the flat response sound pressure level value, and sound level meters have the option of reading levels in dBA as well as dB, dBA being the preferred unit.

6.2.2 B and D-weighting

B-weighting was created to weight sounds at about 70 phons, but it is no longer used. D-weighting was created to weight the noise of aircraft and it is rarely used, while A-weighting is also the common one for aircraft measurements.

6.2.3 C-weighting

This curve is still used by some sound level meters instead of a flat response, but the use of a Z-*weighting* curve is becoming more common to replace the non-weighted measurements. "Z" stands for "zero" weighting.

6.3 Common environmental noise descriptors

WHEN EXTERNAL AND INTERNAL NOISE LEVELS are measured, it is normal for a descriptor to be used which helps to define the period over which the measurement was taken and what part of the measured noise is being assessed. We may simply require an average of the noise level measured over a specific time period (L_{eq}), or we may wish to know what the underlying background noise level is (L_{90}). Listed below are some common noise descriptors used in the measurement of environmental noise.

L_{Aeq}: This is effectively the average measured noise level over a defined period of time. The "A" in the L_{Aeq} parameter means that the noise level has been weighted so that it is akin to the subjective noise level that the average person would hear. The duration is often used to determine an assessment period, the most commonly used are:

$L_{Aeq\,(1hour)}$: A one-hour measurement of the L_{Aeq} often used in daytime industrial noise assessments.

$L_{Aeq\ (16hour)}$: A 16-hour-long measurement of the L_{Aeq} used to describe the period between 7:00 AM and 11:00 PM.

$L_{Aeq\ (8hour)}$: An eight-hour-long measurement of the L_{Aeq} used to describe the period between 11:00 PM and 7:00 AM.

L_{DEN}: A 24-hour-long measurement used to determine the day (7:00 AM–7:00 PM), evening (7:00 PM–11:00 PM), and night (11:00 PM–7:00 AM).

L_{Amax}: The highest single noise event measured over the duration of a survey. Usually associated with a sudden increase in noise such as a train passing

L_{Amin}: The lowest or minimum noise level measured over the duration of a survey. Usually associated with the quietest moment during the survey.

L_{A90}: For some noise sources, such as industrial noise affecting a dwelling, it is common to attempt to control noise in line with the background noise level (L_{A90}). This is the underlying noise level or the average noise level which is exceeded for 90 percent of the measurement period. This allows for noise to be assessed against the quiet periods or lulls in average noise levels, to ensure that a disturbance is not created – i.e., the periods between vehicles passing by a dwelling will result in quiet passages of time where the noise under consideration (industrial noise) may not be masked by other events (road traffic noise) and so cause a disturbance.

L_{A10}: This is the noise level that is exceeded for 10 percent of the duration of the measurement. It is useful for defining noise from road traffic sources, as it focuses on noise when vehicles are passing, rather than including any lulls that may occur between pass-bys. As with L_{Aeq} measurements, the duration of the measurement is often used such as $L_{A10\ (3hour)}$, which can be used for short measurements of road traffic noise or $L_{A10\ (18hour)}$, which can be used for day and evening road traffic measurements used to define the period between 6:00 AM and 12:00 AM.

6.4 Sound insulation performance parameters

DETAILING THE CORRECT PERFORMANCE PARAMETER for separating partitions is an increasingly complex task, due to variations in national requirements, guidance documents, and client specification briefs. Different terms are often used to define acoustic insulation, so, for example, airborne laboratory tests on a sample partition are normally defined as the "STC" in North America and Australasia, while the "R_w" term is more commonly used in Europe.

It is important to know whether airborne sound insulation or impact sound has been measured. As a general rule, any parameter which starts with "STC," "D," or "R" ($D_{n,Tw}$, R'_w, D_w, etc.) will be an airborne sound test, while any parameter which starts with an "IIC/FIIC" or "L" ($L_{n'T,w}$, L_{nw}, ΔL_w) will be an impact sound test.

Simply stating a dB requirement for the acoustic insulation of a partition is inadequate, as it does not describe the method by which the partition is to be assessed and can lead to substantial differences in actual performance (e.g., the difference in on-site performance between specifying a partition with a D_{nTw} of 50 dB compared to a partition with a $D_{nT,w}+C_{tr}$ of 50 dB can be more than 10 dB). Therefore it is necessary to state the performance parameter (STC, $D_{n,Tw}$, R'_w, etc.) as well as the performance criteria (45 dB, 50 dB, etc.).

6.4.1 Commonly used performance parameters

The most commonly used parameters are listed in Table 6.1, which also outlines what they mean and where they are used.

Table 6.1 Most commonly used sound insulation parameters

Parameter	Definition	Commonly used
Airborne sound insulation parameters		
STC	The sound transmission class. Gives a single number value based on the performance of a partition to reduce noise between two rooms across a set range of frequencies (100 Hz to 3150 Hz). The calculated level is adjusted for the effects of room reverberation. (ASTM E90/ASTM E413-10)	North America, New Zealand
FSTC	The field sound transmission class. Gives a single number value based on the performance of the partition to reduce noise across the 100 Hz to 3150 Hz frequency range. The calculated level is adjusted for the effects of room reverberation and background noise.	North America , New Zealand (field testing)
R_w	The weighted sound reduction index of a partition. Gives a single number value based on the performance of a partition to reduce noise	Europe (flanking suppressed lab testing)

Table 6.1 continued

Parameter	Definition	Commonly used
	between two rooms across a set range of frequencies (100 Hz to 3150 Hz). The calculated level is adjusted for the effects of room reverberation and background noise. The calculation takes into account room and partition size. (ISO 140-3 1995/ISO 717-1 1997)	
R'_w	The apparent sound reduction index of a partition. Gives a single number value based on the performance of a partition to reduce noise between two rooms across a set range of frequencies (100 Hz to 3150 Hz). The calculated level is adjusted for the effects of room reverberation. The calculation takes into account the room and partition size. (ISO 140-4 1998/ ISO 717-1 1997)	Europe (flanking laboratory or on-site testing)
ΔR_w	The difference between two measured weighted sound reduction indices. Used to determine the performance of acoustic treatments to a standard core wall or floor. Used to define the performance of acoustic treatments such as floating floor systems. (ISO 140-16 2006/ISO 717 1997)	Europe (flanking suppressed lab testing)
$D_{nT,w}$	The weighted level difference in airborne sound. Used to determine on site performance and measured across the 100 Hz to 3150 Hz frequency range. The result is adjusted for background noise and room reverberation. The result assumes a standard room and partition size. (ISO 140-4 1998/ISO 717-1 1997)	Scotland, Eire, Austria, Belgium (on-site testing)
$D_{nT,w}+C$	The weighted level difference in airborne sound that is then adjusted with a C-weighting spectrum adaptation term to place more emphasis on low frequency performance. Used to determine on-site performance and measured across the 100 Hz to 3150 Hz frequency range. The result is adjusted for background noise and room reverberation. The result assumes a standard room and partition size. (ISO 140-4 1998/ISO 717-1 1997)	France, Switzerland (on-site testing)

| $D_{nT,w}+C_{tr}$ | The weighted level difference in airborne sound that is then adjusted with a C_{tr} spectrum adaptation term to place more emphasis on low frequency performance. Used to determine on-site performance and measured across the 100 Hz to 3150 Hz frequency range. The result is adjusted for background noise and room reverberation. The result assumes a standard room and partition size. (ISO 140-4 1998/ ISO 717-1 1997) | Australia, England, Wales (on-site testing) |
| D_w | The weighted level difference in airborne sound between two rooms. The level is not adjusted for the effects on room reverberation. (ISO 140-4 1998/ISO 717-1 1997) | UK offices, commercial buildings (on-site testing) |

Impact sound insulation parameter

IIC	Impact insulation class. Used to determine the ability of a floor/ceiling to control the transmission of impact or structure-borne noise (e.g., footfall). Measured across the 100 Hz to 3150 Hz frequency band. Only measurements of the noise level in the receiving room are made and so the IIC value is calculated by subtracting the measured level from a base criterion of 110. Hence the larger the IIC value, the better. (ASTM E989-06, 2012/ ASTM E492)	North America, New Zealand (flanking suppressed lab testing)
FIIC	Field impact insulation class. Used to determine the ability of a floor/ceiling to control the transmission of impact or structure-borne noise (e.g., footfall). Measured across the 100 Hz to 3150 Hz frequency band. Only measurements of the noise level in the receiving room are made and so the IIC value is calculated by subtracting the measured level from a base criterion of 110. Hence the larger the IIC value, the better. (ASTM E989-06, (2012)/ASTM E1007-13b)	North America, New Zealand (flanking suppressed lab testing)
L_{nw}	The weighted normalized level from sound being transmitted through a floor or ceiling as a result of impact sound energy being transmitted into the floor using a tapping machine. Measured across the 100 Hz to 3150 Hz frequency band and adjusted for background and room reverberation.	Europe (flanking suppressed lab testing)

Table 6.1 continued

Parameter	Definition	Commonly used
	The calculation takes account of the room and partition size. (ISO 140-6 1998/ISO 717-2 1997)	
L'_{nw}	The weighted normalized level from sound being transmitted through a floor or ceiling as a result of impact sound energy being transmitted into the floor using a tapping machine. Measured across the 100 Hz to 3150 Hz frequency band and adjusted for background and room reverberation. The calculation takes account of the room and partition size. (ISO 140-7 1998/ISO 717-2 1997)	Denmark, Iceland, Italy (on-site testing of floors)
$L'_{nT,w}$	The weighted standardized impact sound pressure level. Used to determine the on-site performance of a floor or ceiling to control impact sound being transmitted from a tapping machine. The level is adjusted for background noise and room reverberation. The calculation assumes a standard room and partition size. (ISO 140-7 1998/ISO 717-2 1997)	Austria, France, UK (on-site testing of floors)
ΔL_w	The difference between two measured weighted normalized level indices. Used to determine the performance of acoustic treatments to a standard core floor. Used to define the performance of acoustic treatments such as floating floor systems. (ISO 140-8 1998/ISO 717-2 1997)	Europe (flanking suppressed lab testing)

Ceilings and small openings

$D_{n,F,w}/D_{nF,n}$	The weighted level difference between two rooms either side of a partition to show the effects of adding a treatment to a flanking element, e.g. a ceiling lining or floor lining. Often quoted by ceiling tile manufacturers. (BS EN 20140-9 1994/ISO 717-1 1997)	Europe (flanking lab testing)
$D_{n,e,w}$	The weighted level difference between two rooms either side of a partition which includes a small test element, e.g. a vent or grill. Indicates the acoustic performance of a small element set into a wall or façade, commonly used to show performance of wall vents. (ISO 20140-10 1992/ISO 717-1 1997)	Europe (flanking suppressed lab testing)

6.4.2 Understanding performance parameters

The level of insulation required is set as a performance criterion and stated in dB. For example, if we were to be undertaking sound insulation testing in dwellings in England and Wales, then the performance parameter is $D_{nT'w+}C_{tr}$ but if we were testing in the United States the performance parameter is likely to be FSTC. In addition to these national variations, there are also differences in the way that sound insulation is defined. As Table 6.1 outlines, there are airborne performance requirements and impact performance requirements. Airborne requirements are set for walls and floors and look at controlling airborne sources such as speech, television, or music noise. Impact performance requirements look at controlling footfall noise created in an upper dwelling in a block of flats or apartments. However, it should be noted that in some countries there are requirements to control horizontal impact sound, e.g., footfall noise from one room to another either side of a wall.

Care should also be taken when applying impact performance requirements. For airborne sound, it is generally the case that the higher the result, the better the wall or floor has performed, but for impact sound there is significant variation dependent on the performance parameter.

Where the terms "IIC" or "ΔL_w" are used, this indicates that the higher the value, the better the performance.

For all other instances ($L'_{nT,w,}$ L'_{nw}), the lower the performance, the better the floor has performed.

Table 6.2 details the perceived relationship between the level of sound insulation offered by a partition and how speech would be perceived in the adjoining room.

It should also be noted that the perceived level of acoustic insulation can be affected by the ambient noise level within a room. Where ambient noise levels in the receiving room are higher, as you may expect in an open plan office or a room next to a busy road, then audible speech from an adjoining room will be limited due to natural masking sound created by other sources. Figure 6.2 shows expected perceived levels for speech from an adjoining room dependent on the insulation of the wall and the steady ambient noise level within the receiving room.

6.4.3 Converting from laboratory testing to on-site testing

It is often necessary to have an idea of how well a total system (i.e., a wall or a floor) will perform when in situ, based on its laboratory performance.

Table 6.2 Perceived relationship between sound insulation values and speech

Description	STC/R_w
Talk at a normal level can be heard and followed in the room next door.	37
Talk at a normal level can be heard and partly distinguished in the room next door.	42
Talk at a normal level can be heard, but words cannot be distinguished in the room next door.	47
Talk at a normal level cannot be heard in the room next door.	52
Loud speech can be heard through the wall but words cannot be distinguished.	57
Loud speech cannot be heard through the wall.	62
Loud shouting can be heard through the wall, but words cannot be distinguished.	67

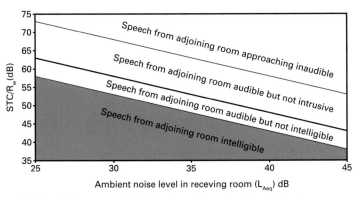

6.2 Relationship between sound insulation of a partition and ambient noise level

The following rules of thumb are normally applied when converting site performance requirements to laboratory performance levels:

Site FSTC = Lab STC −5 dB for masonry partitions
Site FSTC = Lab STC −7 dB for lightweight partitions
Site $D_{nT,w}$ = Lab R_w −5 dB for masonry partitions

Site $D_{nT,w}$ = Lab R_w −7 dB for lightweight partitions

Site $D_{nT,w}$ +C_{tr} = Lab R_w +C_{tr} −10 dB for masonry partitions

Site $D_{nT,w}$ +C_{tr} = Lab R_w +C_{tr} −15 dB for lightweight partitions

6.5 Noise rating

NOISE CRITERIA (NC) CURVES ARE USED in North America, while Noise Rating (NR) Curves are more commonly used in the United Kingdom. Both provide a set of performance values between 63 Hz and 8000 Hz at 1/3 octave bands, which can be used to set performance targets for noise sources that may have a significant frequency component. For example, a fan may have an average noise level L_{Aeq} of 40 dB; however, when each frequency band is considered, it is possible that there is a significant spike in the noise level at, say, 100 Hz. The low noise levels across the other frequency bands therefore average out this spike when considered against an average noise criterion. By

Table 6.3 **Noise criteria and noise rating curves compared**

NR/NC value	1/3 octave band frequencies (Hz)							
	63	125	250	500	1k	2k	4k	8k
NR20	51.3	39.4	30.6	24.3	20.0	16.8	14.4	12.6
NC20	50.5	40.0	33.0	26.5	22.0	19.0	17.0	16.0
NR25	55.2	43.7	35.2	29.2	25.0	21.9	19.5	17.7
NC25	54.0	44.5	37.5	31.0	27.0	24.0	22.0	21.0
NR30	59.2	48.1	39.9	34.0	30.0	26.9	24.7	22.9
NC30	57.0	48.0	41.0	35.5	31.5	29.0	28.0	27.0
NR35	63.1	52.4	44.5	38.9	35.0	32.0	29.8	28.0
NC35	60.5	52.5	45.0	40.0	36.5	34.5	33.0	32.0
NR40	67.1	56.8	49.2	43.8	40.0	37.1	34.9	33.2
NC40	64.0	56.0	50.0	45.0	41.0	39.5	38.5	37.0
NR45	71.0	61.1	53.6	48.6	45.0	42.2	40.0	38.3
NC45	67.0	60.0	54.0	49.0	46.5	44.5	43.0	42.0
NR50	75.0	65.5	58.5	53.5	50.0	47.2	45.2	43.5
NC50	71.0	64.0	58.5	54.0	51.0	49.5	47.5	47.0
NR55	78.9	69.8	63.1	58.4	55.0	52.3	50.3	48.6
NC55	74.0	67.5	62.5	58.5	56.0	54.0	52.5	51.5

setting a performance curve across a frequency range, potentially disturbing noise sources can be identified, controlled, or avoided. NC and NR curves are used primarily when assessing noise from HVAC or noise sources that are likely to have a significant tonal component, such as electrical substations. The aim would be to control noise from a particular source so that it is below the NC or NR criteria at each frequency band. Table 6.3 details the most often used NC and NR curves and compares each set. It should be noted that there are minor differences between NC and NR curves with the same numerical value – for example, NC25 and NR25.

Further reading

Classification for rating sound insulation. ASTM E413-10. West Conshohocken, PA: ASTM.

Standard test method for measurement of airborne sound attenuation between rooms in buildings. ASTM E336-11. West Conshohocken, PA: ASTM.

Standard test method for laboratory measurements of airborne sound transmission loss of building partitions and elements. ASTM E90-09. West Conshohocken, PA: ASTM.

Standard classification for determination of impact insulation class. ASTM E989-06. West Conshohocken, PA: ASTM.

Standard test method for laboratory measurement of impact sound transmission through ceiling assemblies using the tapping machine. ASTM E492-09. West Conshohocken, PA: ASTM.

British Standards Institution (BSI) (1995) *Acoustics. Measurement of sound insulation in buildings and of building elements – Part 3: Laboratory measurements of airborne sound insulation of building elements*. BS EN ISO 140-3. London: BSI.

British Standards Institution (BSI) (1998) *Acoustics. Measurement of sound insulation in buildings and of building elements – Part 4: Field measurements of airborne sound insulation between rooms*. BS EN ISO 140-4. London: BSI.

British Standards Institution (BSI) (1998) *Acoustics. Measurement of sound insulation in buildings and of building elements – Part 8: Laboratory measurements of the reduction of transmitted impact noise by floor coverings on a heavyweight standard floor*. BS EN ISO 140-8. London: BSI.

British Standards Institution (BSI) (2006) *Acoustics – Measurement of sound insulation in buildings and of building elements, Laboratory measurement of sound reduction index improvement by additional linings*. BS EN ISO 140-16. London: BSI.

British Standards Institution (BSI) (1998) *Acoustics. Measurement of sound insulation in building and building elements, Laboratory measurements of impact insulation of floors*. BS EN ISO 140-6. London: BSI.

British Standards Institution (BSI) (1998) *Acoustics. Measurement of sound insulation in buildings and of building elements, Field measurement of impact sound insulation of floors*. BS EN ISO 140- 4. London: BSI.

British Standards Institution (BSI) (1998) *Acoustics. Measurement of sound insulation in buildings and of building elements, Laboratory measurements of transmitted impact noise by floor coverings on a heavyweight standard floor.* BS EN ISO 140-8. London: BSI.

British Standards Institution (BSI) (1994) *Acoustics. Measurement of sound insulation in buildings and of building elements, Laboratory measurement of room to room airborne sound insulation of a suspended ceiling with a plenum above it.* BS EN 20140-9. London: BSI.

British Standards Institution (BSI) (1992) *Acoustics. Measurement of sound insulation in buildings and of building elements, Laboratory measurement of airborne sound insulation of small building elements.* BS EN 20140-10. London: BSI.

British Standards Institution (BSI) (1997) *Acoustics, Rating of sound insulation in buildings and building elements, airborne sound insulation.* BS EN ISO 717-1. London: BSI.

British Standards Institution (BSI) (1997) *Acoustics, Rating of sound insulation in buildings and building elements, impact sound insulation.* BS EN ISO 717-2. London: BSI.

British Standards Institution (BSI) (1997) *Acoustics, Sound absorbers for use in buildings, rating of sound absorption.* BS EN ISO 11654. London: BSI.

COST (2013) *Towards a common framework in building acoustics throughout Europe. European Conference on Sound Insulation in Housing: Findings of COST Action TU0901*, Copenhagen, December 3.

Part II

Applications

chapter 7

Educational buildings

7.1 The importance of good acoustics in educational building design

THERE CAN BE FEW BUILDING TYPES where acoustic design plays such a key role in the success of the people who use the building. A review of 30 years' worth of international research (Shield & Dockrell, 2003) highlighted that acoustics in the classroom can impact on student memory retention and concentration levels. The research shows that the acoustic environment can alter performance in mathematics, problem solving, reading ability, language skills, and impact on literacy levels. It should be noted that these studies are on children classified as having standard hearing ability. The need for social inclusion of children with hearing impairments and special educational needs only increases potential for poor acoustic design to adversely affect performance.

Research (Canning & James, 2012) has also shown that applying standards normally associated with special teaching facilities for hearing impaired children can have a significant effect on educational attainment, behavior, and even teacher and student comfort. Therefore it is worth considering the application of higher standards rather than aiming to achieve a basic level of performance.

The following section provides general good practices for the design of school buildings looking at the control of reverberation, noise disturbance, and speech intelligibility.

7.2 Performance criteria

7.2.1 Performance specifications

The aim of any acoustic design for an educational building is to minimize the likelihood of disruption to the students, make it as easy as possible for the students to hear the teacher and each other, and as easy as possible for the teacher to hear the students.

To achieve this, the acoustic design of any educational building will look at three key factors:

- controlling noise break-in from external sources (location, orientation, façade, roof, and ventilation design)
- controlling the transfer of sound within the school (layout, partition, detailing design, HVAC design)
- controlling the reverberation time within a school (room size, room shape, room finishes)

7.2.2 Signal to Noise Ratio (SNR)
Table 7.1 details accepted good guidelines with regards to signal to noise ratios in classrooms.

7.2.3 External noise limits
Controlling noise within schools grounds is important; these areas can be used for teaching activities. Table 7.2 outlines suitable external noise limits around a school.

Where measurements indicate that noise levels on a proposed school site are below L_{Aeq} 45 dB, then this can be seen as a positive indication that no mitigation work would be required to protect either the external or internal teaching areas. Where noise levels exceed the values expressed in Table 7.2, external mitigation work may be necessary.

Table 7.1 Good practice guidelines on signal to noise ratios for teaching rooms (adapted from EFA, 2012)

Standard	Description	Signal to Noise
Minimum	For students without hearing impairment or Special Education Needs (SEN)	>10 dB
Basic	For all students, including hearing impaired and SEN	>15 dB
Enhanced	For all students including hearing impaired and SEN	>20 dB 125 Hz–750 Hz >15 dB 750 Hz–4 kHz

Table 7.2 Permissible upper noise limits for external space around a school (adapted from DoE, 2004)

Location	Permissible upper limit L_{Aeq} (dB)
Noise level at proposed school façade	60 dB
Outdoor area used for informal teaching	60 dB
Outdoor recreation areas	60 dB
Playing fields/sports fields (unoccupied)	55 dB
Outdoor formal teaching	50 dB

7.2.4 Doors between teaching spaces and circulation areas

For schools it is accepted that the level of sound insulation for corridor walls separating rooms from circulation spaces which have doors or glazing in them would not be testable on site. Therefore a performance criterion based on laboratory performance should be set. This means that laboratory test data can be used as evidence that a partition specification is suitable for use.

For all rooms to circulation spaces except music rooms, a minimum standard would be STC/R_w 40 dB for the wall and STC/R_w 30 dB for the door set.

For music rooms to circulation spaces, a minimum standard would be STC/R_w 45 dB for the wall and STC/R_w 35 dB for the door.

7.2.5 Internal openings

Table 7.3 provides guidance on suitable performance levels for doors, roller doors to server hatches, demountable partitions, and glazed screens for vision panels.

7.3 Design guidelines

7.3.1 Controlling external noise

When considering the location and positioning of a school, consideration must be given to providing quiet external areas as well as ensuring quiet internal areas.

Minimum distances between educational buildings and transportation noise sources: It is considered best practice to locate schools 328 ft (100 m) from any busy road or railway line; however, it is anticipated that achieving these

Table 7.3 Suggested performance requirements for openings in internal walls

Opening type	Suggested specification	Expected Performance rating STC/ Rw dB	Suitable location
Serving hatch	100 mm galvanized steel slats minimum surface density of 50 kg/m^2	25	• Serving hatch between kitchen and dining halls
Operable/ movable wall	Particle board clad in vinyl/fabric/veneer, etc. either side of steel frame with mineral fiber insulation infill. Nominal 64 kg/m2 hanging weight	52	• Drama studio to other teaching space • Between sports halls • Between multipurpose halls/ dining halls
Standard door	Timber/metal door (light 44 mm @ 27 kg/m^2)	30	• Standard teaching spaces to corridor • Ancillary rooms to corridor
Enhanced door	Timber/metal door (heavy 54 mm @ 29 kg/ m^2)	35	• Music rooms to corridor • Control rooms to corridor • Drama rooms to corridor • Multipurpose halls to corridor • Rooms for children with special hearing or communication needs to corridor` • Interconnecting door standard teaching spaces
Optimum door	Back-to-back timber/ metal door (heavy 54 mm @ 29 kg/m^2)	40	• Interconnecting music rooms
Unrated vision panel	Single layer of glass in sliding frame	n/a	• Where visual and verbal communication is required, e.g.

Opening type	Suggested specification	Expected Performance rating STC/ Rw dB	Suitable location
			reception desk to waiting room
Standard vision panel	10mm float glass/12 mm cavity/6.4 mm laminate glass	40	• Glazing set into a corridor wall or door frame between a standard teaching space and circulation space
Enhanced vision panel	6mm float glass/100 mm cavity/4 mm float glass	45	• Where visual communication is required between teaching spaces e.g. teaching space to multipurpose hall
Optimum vision panel	10 mm float glass/200 mm cavity/6 mm laminated glass (absorptive lining to window reveal between panes of glass)	49	• Between music rooms/recording studio and control rooms
Through wall ventilator	2 m² open area vent with 50 percent open, 50 percent open-cell foam, minimum length 1.1 m	$D_{ne,w}$ 39dB	• Cross-ventilation via corridor walls

sorts of distances in urban locations will be difficult. Standoff distance between schools and busy roads of 65 ft (20 m), and 98 ft (30 m) between schools and railway lines, should be seen as an absolute minimum. Locating the building closer increases the likelihood for vibration and reradiated sound becoming a problem. It should be noted that at these minimum distances noise from a road or railway is likely to still be a significant issue and will need to be controlled.

Aircraft noise has been cited as a factor in poor educational attainment and is a particular issue for external teaching spaces. Efforts should be made to ensure that schools are not constructed in an area where airport noise contours exceed daytime average of L_{Aeq} 56 dB. Where formal outdoor teaching is necessary, the use of gazebos or pavilions can help to reduce aircraft noise levels but only where the surface mass of the roof and wall structures exceeds 15 kg/m².

Barriers can help reduce noise levels within external areas and benefit noise control at the façade of the school. Guidelines on barrier design are given in Chapter 4. It is possible to use the school building to create an acoustic barrier between the noise source and the required external area. Horseshoe- or L-shaped buildings which form a protected square are an effective means of creating quiet zones around the school. Barriers built in front of a building are only likely to be effective up to first-floor level where noise sources are near the ground (roads, railways, some industrial activities).

Sports fields associated with the school can cause noise problems for the school and surrounding dwellings, particularly if they are used outside normal school hours (e.g., formal evening football games). The following good practices should be considered when designing outdoor sports fields:

■ Try to locate formal sports fields, or sports fields which are for evening or community use, as far from existing dwellings as possible. Complaints from dwellings which are up to 328 ft (100 m) from the sports field are possible.

■ The construction of a barrier with an effective height of 6 ft 6 in–8 ft 2 in (2.0–2.5 m) along the boundary of the school grounds where it adjoins the property line of a dwelling can reduce noise impact where there is a clear line of sight between the sports field and the garden (yard) of the dwelling. The barrier should have a minimum surface mass of 15 kg/m².

■ Orienting sports fields so that bleacher seating breaks any line of sight between nearby dwellings and the playing surface can help reduce noise impact.

■ Noise from a ball striking a boundary fence can be a cause for complaints and so nets may be a better option.

■ Management of such facilities is paramount. If noise disturbance is likely, then the frequency and type of evening or weekend events should be limited.

7.3.2 Minimizing noise break-in from external sources

Controlling noise break-in is dependent upon the façade design and the roof construction. There is a growing preference for naturally ventilated buildings, which can be at odds with acoustic requirements, as open windows or open ventilation normally mean limited options to control noise. Chapter 4 details the expected performance levels for a number of façade and roof constructions.

Building layout offers an obvious means of control as locating noise-sensitive rooms away from high noise areas can limit the need for enhanced façade specifications. Rooms to be used for hearing-impaired children or children with special educational needs should be priorities so that their location is away from any noisy external activity (e.g. busy roads/railway lines).

Effort should be made to locate the following room types away from areas of high noise (e.g., roads/railway lines):

- nursery/kindergarten rooms
- elementary/primary classrooms
- teaching and tutorial rooms
- music rooms
- lecture rooms
- drama studios
- assembly halls.

Figure 7.1 outlines a simple design layout for a large school where road noise is an issue.

1) Courtyard areas which are protected from road traffic noise and so could be suitable for outside formal teaching.
2) Location of most noise-sensitive rooms furthest from main noise source (road). The wing arrangement for 2, 3, and 4 means that noisy and quiet activities can be split.
3) Suitable for standard teaching activities, still shielded from road noise.
4) Suitable for least noise-sensitive activities, such as ancillary space or workshops. Even here the more noise-sensitive spaces can be built along the façade which faces away from the road.
5) Suitable for circulation or atrium space as well as sports facilities.
6) Can be used for dining space.

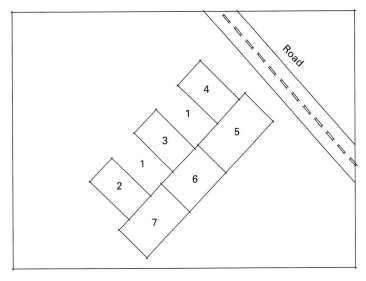

7.1 Possible building layout where road noise is an issue

7) Good location for assembly or large lecture theaters as well as large drama space.

7.3.3 Façade design

Natural ventilation from open windows and/or acoustically untreated vents can be used if:

- windows are top- or bottom-hung and have a restricted opening of no more than 4 in (100 mm);
- external noise levels at the façade are not 13 dB higher than the required internal ambient noise level when the intake and outlet of any vent are in the same façade;

or

- external noise levels at the façade are not more than 18 dB where the intake is in the façade exposed to the noise and the outlet vent is located on another elevation (e.g. to a ventilation stack or cross ventilation system);

or

■ external ambient noise levels do not exceed an absolute level of L_{Aeq} of 40 dB.

The +13 dB or +18 dB recommendations means that if the noise level is measured at the proposed façade position prior to the building being constructed, and it is found to be around L_{Aeq} 48 dB, then untreated natural ventilation should be suitable for any room where the upper indoor ambient noise limit is L_{Aeq} 35 dB (see Appendix B for details of ambient noise limits by room type). In some instances it may be allowable to increase this level by +5 dB due to a tradeoff in performance requirements between acoustics and natural ventilation. *Note*: Even with the tradeoff, these are low ambient noise levels for an urban environment.

Natural ventilation for fixed glazing and acoustically treated vents is possible even in high noise areas and where the most stringent performance requirements are set, such as classrooms for hearing-impaired children. Achieving suitable noise control is normally associated with significant detailing of vents. Figure 7.2 shows a natural ventilation specification that was successfully used to control noise break-in from road traffic in a special educational needs school.

Cross-flow natural ventilation and natural stack ventilation is often used to vent air that may be drawn in through the main façade and can cause acoustic issues. Figure 7.3 details good practices:

1) Ventilate at high level above corridor to external environment to avoid noise transfer from teaching space to circulation space.

2) Natural cross-ventilation into corridors will require significant attenuation. A lined duct longer than 39 in (1 m) in length is likely to be required. Greater ventilation requirements or multiple ducts will mean greater attenuation is needed. A continuous duct across the corridor could be a suitable alternative to avoid cross-talk.

3) Natural ventilation ducts to the roof should never be shared between floors to avoid cross-talk issues. Where ducts from lower floors pass through upper rooms lagging with 25 mm quilt and lining with x2 layers

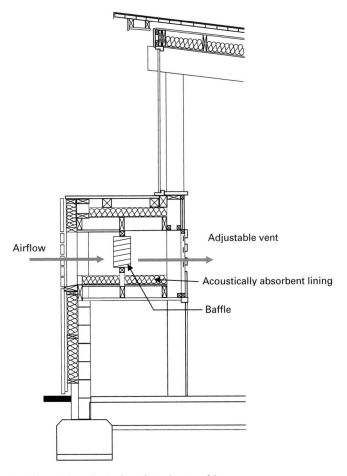

Airflow

Adjustable vent

Acoustically absorbent lining

Baffle

7.2 Through-the-wall natural ventilation (not to scale)

plasterboard/dryline on, an independent frame will be needed. Ducts should be kept independent of each other.

4) Ventilation into a ceiling void within a corridor can be a suitable option assuming a plasterboard ceiling with a minimum surface density of 12 kg/m^2 is used.

(see Figure 7.3)

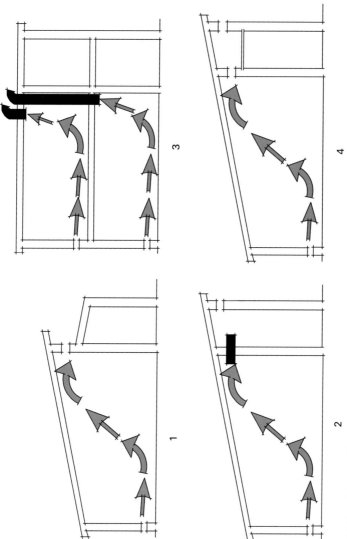

7.3 Natural cross-ventilation

Rain noise through roof structures can generally be assumed to be controlled where noise from heavy rain fall does not cause the targeted ambient noise level (Appendix B) within a room to increase by more than 20 dB.

7.3.4 Room layout and adjacencies

The following room adjacencies should be avoided in any school design:

- music rooms to workshops
- music rooms to sensory-impaired rooms
- music rooms to medical rooms
- music rooms to nursery/kindergarten
- sports halls to sensory-impaired rooms.

When considering layout, it is best to cluster like activities together, as suggested in Figure 7.1.

Within groupings, some rooms will have expected high noise activity levels and so it can be useful to detail store rooms between rooms to act as a buffer (e.g., placing a store between two music practice rooms).

Use ancillary space such as bathroom blocks or staff rooms to create buffer zones between grouped activities (e.g., locating ancillary space to the entrance of a wing of a building with the teaching space placed in the middle and end of the wing). This also helps to locate teaching activity away from primary circulation and social spaces.

Locate rooms with high use or high occupancy levels (e.g., large lecture theaters) closer to primary circulation routes, to reduce unnecessary footfall along corridors.

Rooms used for sensitive discussions, such as headteachers' offices, medical rooms, or counseling rooms, should be situated away from primary circulation routes, to avoid eavesdropping.

Locate machine rooms away from teaching rooms. Ideally they should be located in a separate building outside the main school building.

7.3.5 Services through walls

Puncturing separating walls with electrical and mechanical services will have a detrimental effect on the acoustic performance of the partition. The following approach should be adopted:

■ Where the required performance is below STC/R$_w$ 50 dB and there is no ceiling, it is possible to allow for electrical cables or pipework to pass through a wall separating two rooms, assuming the number of penetrations is limited (two or three) and each penetration is no more than 9 sq/in (25 mm^2).

■ Where the required performance is between STC/R$_w$ 50 dB and STC/R$_w$ 57 dB, it is possible to allow for electrical cables or pipework to pass through a wall separating two rooms assuming the number of penetrations is limited (two or three), each penetration is no more than 9 sq/in (25 mm^2), and they are located above a mineral fiber tile ceiling.

■ For partitions where the performance requirement is above STC/R$_w$, 57 dB all service penetrations should be avoided.

■ Large duct service penetrations (e.g., ventilation or heating ducts) should always be taken via a corridor wall, as indicated in Figure 7.4.

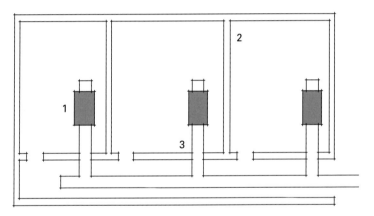

7.4 Correct method for large M&E services

1) Use of attenuator before the duct grill required to reduce possible issues from cross-talk. Additional cross-talk attenuators may be necessary along the main duct.

2) Partition has no large penetrations, thereby maintaining the acoustic integrity of the partition.

3) Service penetration taken through corridor wall, which is less acoustically sensitive.

7.3.6 Room finishes

Table 7.4 outlines suggested wall, floor, and ceiling finishes to ensure the control of reverberation and good speech intelligibility within a range of educational accommodation, α_w are given for ceiling and wall panel finishes. Examples of suitable materials would be mineral fiber ceiling tiles, fabric-covered foam, fiber-backed panels, or perforated timber veneer acoustic panels (see Appendix C for a list of suitable finishes).

Table 7.4 Recommended floor, wall, and ceiling finishes by material and absorption coefficient α_w (education)

Room description	Floor α_w	Ceiling finish α_w	Wall α_w
Any classroom/ tutorial with carpeted floor	0.3 Carpet	0.8 over full ceiling (allowance for lighting)	Plaster finish
Any classroom/ tutorial with vinyl floor	Unrated	0.9 over full ceiling (allowance for lighting)	0.8 evenly spread over 15 percent side and rear walls
Classroom for hearing-impaired children or special educational needs children	0.3 Carpet	0.9 suspended grid tile ceiling over ceiling (allowance for lighting) with an additional 100 mm mineral fiber quilt above tiles	0.9 evenly spread over 20 percent side and rear walls
Art rooms	Vinyl flooring (unrated)	0.9 over ceiling (allowance for lighting)	0.8 evenly spread over 15% of side and rear walls
Assembly halls/ multipurpose halls	Vinyl flooring (unrated)	0.9 over full ceiling (allowance for lighting)	0.8 evenly spread over 25 percent of side walls and 60 percent of available area to rear walls
Atria/social interaction space	Vinyl flooring (unrated)	Glass to main atrium, 0.9 to any exposed ceiling above walkways and circulation routes	0.9 evenly spread over 60% of total wall area, include balustrades and bulkheads if available
Changing rooms	Vinyl flooring (unrated)	0.8 over full ceiling area (allowance for lighting)	Plaster or tile

Room description	Floor αw	Ceiling finish αw	Wall αw
Corridors/ stairwells/ cloakrooms	Vinyl flooring (unrated)	0.9 over full ceiling area (allowance for lighting)	Plaster or painted brick/block
Dance studio	Timber	0.9 over full ceiling area (allowance for lighting)	0.8 evenly spread over 25 percent of all walls
Dining rooms	Vinyl or hard surface (unrated)	0.8 over full ceiling	0.8 over 30 percent of wall area
Drama studio	Vinyl flooring (unrated)	0.8 over full ceiling area (allowance for lighting)	Theater curtain set 50–100 mm from wall in folds over at least three walls
Gymnasium	Vinyl flooring/ Timber (unrated)	Perforated metal deck over full ceiling area min 30% perforations with mineral fiber quilt behind	Fair faced unpainted block to 3m. Remaining wall area above lined with 0.8 absorptive panels
Kitchens	Vinyl/tile (unrated)	0.8 over full ceiling area	Plaster or tile
Language labs	0.3 Carpet	0.8 over full ceiling (allowance for lighting)	Plaster finish
Lecture room large >50 students	0.3 Carpet	0.8 over rear 75 percent of ceiling	0.8 over 25 percent of wall distributed over the back wall and the rear of the side walls
Lecture room small <50 students	0.3 Carpet	0.8 over 50 percent of ceiling	0.8 over 25 percent of walls located to rear of room
Library quiet space	0.3 Carpet	0.9 over full ceiling (allowance for lighting)	Plaster finish
Library resource space	0.3 Carpet	0.9 over full ceiling (allowance for lighting)	0.9 evenly spread over 15 percent side and rear walls
Meeting/interview/ counseling	0.3 Carpet	0.8 over 50% of ceiling	0.8 over 25 percent of wall area
Music ensemble room	0.3 Carpet	Plasterboard	Theater curtain set 50 mm from wall in folds

Table 7.4 continued

Room description	Floor αw	Ceiling finish αw	Wall αw
			over at least three walls that can be pulled back to expose plaster or block walls
Music group practice room >30m³	0.3 Carpet	0.8 over full ceiling (allowance for lighting)	Plaster finish
Music group practice room <30m³	0.3 Carpet	0.8 over full ceiling (allowance for lighting)	Plaster finish
Music performance/ recital room	0.3 Carpet	Plasterboard	Theater curtain set 50 mm from wall in folds over at least three walls that can be pulled back to expose plaster or block walls
Music room (elementary/ primary)	0.3 Carpet	0.8 over full ceiling (allowance for lighting)	Plaster finish
Music room (middle/high/ secondary)	0.3 Carpet	0.8 over full ceiling (allowance for lighting)	Plaster finish
Offices/medical rooms/staff rooms	0.3 Carpet	0.8 over full ceiling (allowance for lighting)	Plaster finish
Open plan breakout areas	0.3 Carpet	0.9 over full ceiling (allowance for lighting)	0.8 over 15 percent of wall area
Open plan teaching space	0.3 Carpet	0.9 over full ceiling (allowance for lighting)	0.9 over 15 percent of wall area
Recording studio	0.3 Carpet	0.9 over full ceiling (allowance for lighting)	Plaster
Recording studio control room	0.3 Carpet	0.9 over full ceiling (allowance for lighting)	0.8 over 15 percent of available wall area
Science laboratories	Vinyl unrated	0.8 over full ceiling (allowance for lighting)	Plaster/painted block finish

Room description	Floor &w	Ceiling finish &w	Wall &w
Sports halls	Vinyl flooring/ timber (unrated)	Perforated metal deck with fiber quilt behind over full ceiling area	Fair faced unpainted block to 3 m. Remaining wall area above lined with 0.8 absorptive panels
Study room (individual or withdrawn study)	0.3 Carpet	0.8 over full ceiling (allowance for lighting)	Plaster finish
Swimming pools	Tile (unrated)	Perforated metal liner tray over full ceiling area min 30 percent perforations with mineral fibre quilt behind or 0.7 moisture resistant absorptive tiles	Fair-faced block
Teaching kitchens, electronics, textile, ICT	Vinyl (unrated)	0.9 over full ceiling (allowance for lighting)	Plaster/painted block finish
Toilets/showers	Vinyl flooring (unrated)	0.8 over full ceiling area (allowance for lighting and moisture resistant ceiling to shower cubicles)	Plaster or tiles
Workshops (metal/ woodworking/ machine)	Vinyl (unrated)	0.9 over full ceiling (allowance for lighting)	Plaster/painted block finish plus 0.8 wall panels at high level in 600 mm deep band around room perimeter

Specification details for good practice when constructing separating walls and floors is given in the drawings in Appendix C.

7.3.7 Music departments

The room type within a music department will dictate its design. Guidelines on good layouts are outlined below.

- Large performance spaces (e.g., halls/recital) – should be typically 279 ft^2 (85 m^2) in size, with ceiling heights of up to 19 ft (6 m), and have a rectangular floor plan.
- General teaching space – typically 213 sq/ft (65 m^2) with 10 ft (3 m) floor-to-ceiling height with a rectangular floor plan.
- Ensemble rooms – typically 65 ft^2 (20 m^2) with 10 ft (3 m) floor-to-ceiling height with non-parallel walls.
- Practice rooms – typically 26 ft^2 (8 m^2) with 10 ft (3 m) floor-to-ceiling height with non-parallel walls.
- Control rooms – typically 32 ft^2 (10 m^2) with 10 ft (3 m) floor-to-ceiling height and rectangular in shape.

Figure 7.5 outlines some methods for providing non-parallel walls within ensemble or practice rooms.

1) Option 1: construct wall at an angle.
2) Option 2: construct straight walls, then construct false wall with plasterboard and stud work.
3) Option 3: construct room with straight walls and line with shaped timber, foam, or fiber wall-mounted panels.

(see Figure 7.5, opposite)

7.3.8 Music room walls and ceilings

High levels of acoustic insulation are required between music rooms and between music rooms and other teaching spaces. It is commonly necessary to adopt the following:

- Absolutely no service penetrations through any wall which separates a music room from another music room or teaching space.
- For walls with a minimum specification of STC/R$_w$ 60 dB, a suspended plasterboard ceiling or a suspended acoustically absorptive ceiling with plasterboard backing is required. This is to control flanking transmission at the wall head as well as sound transmission to any rooms above.
- Double layers of plasterboard to flanking walls are likely to be necessary (e.g., external and corridor walls).

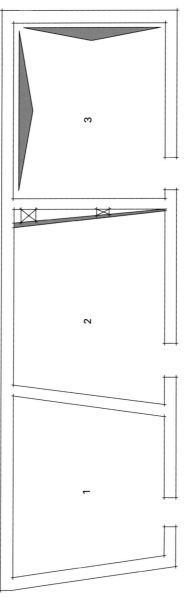

7.5 Non-standard-shape music practice rooms

7.3.9 Open-plan teaching

It should be understood that the effectiveness of open-plan teaching is as reliant on the adoption of particular teaching methods as it is on the design of the space. A client who desires a building with open-plan teaching space should also be fully ready to adopt the teaching methods associated with this type of space. Acoustic design can only go so far, with the management of the space being the primary means of noise control. Timetable and activity management should be part of the design process.

The two main aims in open-plan teaching are to ensure that: 1) disturbance from other activities is limited in areas where group listening occurs; and 2) the buildup of noise is controlled in areas where interactive work occurs.

General good design for open-plan teaching is outlined below:

- Limiting floor to ceiling heights to 11 ft (3.50 m). A variable ceiling height can help to reduce problematic sound reflections.
- Introduce bulkhead details (i.e., sections of wall extending down from the ceiling to just above head height) to delineate between different teaching areas and help reduce noise transfer (e.g., at the entrance to a teaching space or above a designated quiet area).
- Placing acoustic screens between activity areas should be considered. Screen heights of 5 ft 2 in –6 ft 6 in (1.6–2 m) are recommended. Screens should have acoustically absorptive finishes either side and should have a minimum mass per unit area of $12 kg/m^2$.
- Flat lens-style lighting or lighting set behind a flat Perspex or glazed panel should be avoided, to minimize unwanted reflections.
- Locate areas for groups listening to a single teacher as far apart as possible. Areas for interactive work or areas for non-private individual teacher–student discussion can be clustered together and used to form buffer zones between intense listening zones.
- The inclusion of movable walls should be considered, particularly where it is anticipated that there will be clashes between activity areas with regards to signal to noise ratios or speech intelligibility, i.e., where it may not be possible to provide sufficient distance between activity groups.
- For traditional chalk and talk activities, reduce the distance between teacher and student with compact seating arrangements or even raked seating.

- Open-plan teaching areas should not be directly linked or open out into atrium or large dining areas.
- The number of individual classes or activities per open-plan space should be limited to two to three classes in primary/elementary schools and three to four classes in other teaching environments.
- A Speech Transmission Index of >0.6 is suggested as a suitable target for areas designed for group listening, or where hearing-impaired children or children with special educational needs are taught.
- A Speech Transmission index of <0.4 is suggested between activity groups.

Further reading

Canning, D., and James, A. (2012) *The Essex Study: Optimised Classroom Acoustics for all*. St Albans: Association of Noise Consultants.

Crandell C. C., and Smaldino, J. J. (2000) Classroom acoustics for children with normal hearing and with hearing impairment. *Language, Speech and Hearing Services in Schools*, 31: 362–370 (American Speech-Language-Hearing Association).

DoE (2004) *Building Bulletin 93: Acoustic design of schools, a design guide 2004*. London: Department for Education.

EFA (2012) Acoustic performance standards for the Priority Schools Building Programme 2012, London: Education Funding Agency.

Jaramillo, A. M., and Ermann, M. G. (2013) The link between HCAV type and student achievement. Unpublished doctoral dissertation, Virginia Tech, VA.

Mathews, D., and Mangan, A. (2001) *Guidelines for mainstream teachers with deaf pupils in their class*. Education guidelines project. London: RNID.

Scottish Executive (2007) *School Design: Optimising Internal Environments; Building our future, Scotland's School Estates*. Edinburgh: Scottish Executive.

Seep, B., Glosemeyer, R., Hulce, E., Linn, M., Aytar P., and Coffeen, B. (2000) *Classroom acoustics, a resource for creating learning environments with desirable listening conditions*. New York: Acoustical Society of America.

Shield, Bridget M., and Dockrell, Julie E. (2003) The effects of noise on children at school: A review. *Journal of Building Acoustics* 10(2): 97–106.

chapter 8

Healthcare

8.1 The importance of good acoustics in healthcare design

NOISE IS OFTEN AN UNWANTED STIMULUS to the body, and clear links have been established between prolonged exposure to noise and shorter life expectancy (Maynard & Moorhouse, 2009). Good acoustic design is often seen as simply controlling disturbance and maintaining privacy. In healthcare buildings, good acoustic design is of greater importance because it can affect the health and recovery of the patients using the building. High noise levels not only cause obvious effects like annoyance and sleep disturbance but also decrease the rate at which patients' wounds heal and increase the likelihood of rehospitalization. Links have also been found between noise exposure of staff and increased levels of stress, fatigue, and emotional exhaustion (Anjali & Ulrich, 2007). This is in addition to the usual communication difficulties associated with any noisy environment.

With regards to privacy there are few environments where maintaining confidentiality is of such importance. Architects and designers in the US should be aware that it is a federal government requirement to ensure that healthcare organizations provide privacy for patient health information. This extends to any spoken information and so it becomes directly linked to the acoustic performance of the building.

8.2 Performance criteria

8.2.1 Performance specifications

Healthcare buildings are often unique in their acoustic requirements due to the very nature of the building's use. With high levels of mechanical and electrical services, controlling noise from the building becomes a particular issue.

Much of the machinery and many tasks undertaken within healthcare buildings require controlled environments and this often extends to the control of noise and even vibration. Finally, providing privacy, confidentiality, and comfort are paramount but often conflict with the nature and use of the building.

The three key design goals for healthcare buildings are as follows:

- controlling noise affecting patient and staff areas from either external noise sources or noise sources associated with the building,
- providing partitions within the building that will ensure that confidentiality is maintained, as well as enhancing the control of possible noise disturbance,
- providing suitable levels of control with regards to room acoustics without compromising clinical standards and performance.

Specific guideline levels for airborne sound insulation, ambient noise control, acceptable mechanical noise levels, and impact insulation requirements are detailed in Appendix B.

8.2.2 Sound insulation

With specific regards to sound insulation of partitions:

- Locating rooms adjacent to one another that result in a minimum partition requirement of STC/R_w of 64 dB should be avoided.
- For long-term health care facilities, e.g., residential care, performance specifications for walls and floors should be in line with local building codes/standards associated with separating partitions between dwellings.
- It should be remembered that loud speech is not uncommon in treatment and consultation rooms, so good levels of acoustic insulation are of paramount importance if privacy is to be protected.

8.2.3 Controlling reverberation

Reverberation times are not commonly set as performance standards in healthcare buildings, due to often conflicting clinical requirements. It is considered good practice to ensure that:

- An area equivalent to 80 percent of the floor should be covered with a material which provides a minimum NRC/absorption coefficient of 0.95.

■   Where this cannot be achieved the acoustic performance of any separating partition either side of the room should be increased by 3 dB.

An absorption coefficient of 0.15 is required for most patient treatment or clinical areas (e.g., plaster walls, vinyl flooring). A higher average absorption coefficient of 0.25 is suggested for waiting areas to reduce noise build up.

For non-clinical areas, such as administrative or conference accommodation, guidelines for offices or educational buildings can be followed. Large open atrium or circulation areas are likely to require specialized acoustic design.

8.2.4 External noise limits

External areas used by staff, patients, or the public, such as accessible courtyards or landscaped areas, should be designed so that noise from services associated with the hospital does not exceed the existing daytime background level (L_{A90}) or is not higher than L_{A90} 50 dB, whichever is highest.

When considering the design of mental healthcare facilities, it is not unusual for the location to be chosen based on the tranquil nature of the existing environment. For outdoor treatment or relaxation areas, upper average noise limits of L_{Aeq} 50–55 dB during the daytime should be targeted.

Mechanical noise from the healthcare building should be controlled to a level which does not exceed L_{Aeq} 65 dB at the healthcare building façade and controlled to the pre-existing ambient noise level at the nearest noise sensitive location (e.g. dwelling), whichever is lowest.

Heliports should be located such that noise levels do not exceed L_{Aeq} 80 dB at the nearest noise sensitive location (e.g., dwelling). This assumes limited use of the heliport, i.e., fewer than three flights per day and no more than two flights during the nighttime period (10:00 PM–7:00 AM).

Emergency generator noise should be controlled to a level of L_{Aeq} 70 dB when measured at the façade of the healthcare building.

8.2.5 Internal doors and openings

Table 8.1 outlines suggested performance requirements for openings in internal walls, along with specification information and suitable locations. Doors to store cupboards and similar ancillary space would not require an acoustically rated door.

Table 8.1 **Suggested performance requirements for openings in walls**

Opening type	Suggested specification	Expected performance rating STC/ R_w dB	Suitable location
Standard door	Timber/metal door (light 44 mm @ 27 kg/m²)	30	• Staff offices, meeting rooms, etc. to corridors • Ancillary rooms to corridors
Enhanced door	Timber/metal door (heavy 54 mm @ 29 kg/m²)	35	• Any medical treatment or consultation rooms to corridors or adjoining space
Unrated vision panel	Single layer of glass in sliding frame	n/a	• Where visual and verbal communication is required, e.g., reception desk to waiting room
Standard vision panel	10 mm float glass/12 mm cavity/6.4 mm laminate glass	40	• Glazing set into a corridor wall or door frame between a medical treatment space and circulation space where some verbal communication is required
Enhanced vision panel	6mm float glass/100 mm cavity/4 mm float glass	45	• Where visual communication is required between a medical treatment space and another room, e.g., operating theater to observation gallery
Optimum vision panel	10 mm float glass/200 mm cavity/6 mm laminated glass (absorptive lining to window reveal between panes of glass)	49	• Between highly noise-sensitive areas and adjoining spaces, e.g., infant ICU and visitor gallery or treatment and observation rooms

Door seals are advisable for acoustic reasons but may conflict with the control of the spread of infections or operational suitability, for these reasons:

■ Rubberized seals are likely to be more clinically suitable than felt or brush seals.
■ Infection control designers should be consulted on the use of door seals.
■ It may not be possible to accommodate seals in doors which swing both ways or double doors, as compressible seals may require a rebate.
■ Drop-down seals are likely to cause issues for rooms where trolley access is required.

8.2.6 Maximum permissible noise levels

Noise intrusion from external sources and noise from other parts of the building should be controlled to below $L_{Amax(f)}$ 45 dB within rooms where patients may be sleeping, and $L_{Amax(f)}$ 50 dB for operating rooms.

8.3 Design guidelines

8.3.1 Controlling external noise

Heliports: Figure 8.1 details the suggested positioning for a hospital heliport, assuming it is located on the ground. For heliports located on the roof of a hospital, it would be necessary to ensure that no treatment/consultant rooms, patient sleeping areas, operating rooms or noise-sensitive laboratory equipment is located on the floor directly below the heliport and any room within 20 ft (6 m) of the helipad. Where possible, heliports should be located on top of ancillary space such as mechanical rooms and as remote from the core healthcare activities as possible. Specialist guidance on façade and roof specifications should be sought for roof-mounted heliports.

1) Nearest dwelling or noise-sensitive location
2) Minimum slant distance between noise-sensitive location and helicopter
3) Helicopter takeoff flight path
4) Helipad
5) Hospital
6) Minimum standoff distance between heliport and hospital building

(see Figure 8.1)

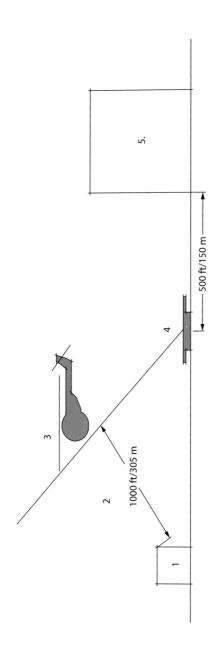

8.1 Heliport location

Road and rail noise: It is advisable to ensure that any rooms specifically for the treatment or care of patients, along with any noise-sensitive rooms (e.g., operating rooms), are a minimum of 65 ft (20 m) from any road or railway line. Control of noise break-in to such areas will be reliant upon design; therefore it is likely that mechanical ventilation will be required as allowing for open windows for ventilation would not be an option. The general principles on building location and layouts outlined in Chapter 4 and Chapter 7 should be consulted.

Courtyards are often a popular design feature of healthcare developments due to the size of the building. These can provide quiet areas around which noise-sensitive rooms can be clustered and allow for natural ventilation to rooms. In such areas, the following is advised:

- Windows should be top-hinged, bottom-hinged, or sash and case opening to limit noise ingress and reduce noise egress from a room.
- If the courtyards are to be accessible to staff, patients or visitors, placing noise-sensitive rooms or rooms where patient privacy is important at ground-floor level, should be avoided.
- Placing seating directly against the façade of any courtyard should be avoided, to maintain privacy to rooms which overlook the space.
- The use of dense soft planting and soft landscaping should be encouraged in order to limit noise buildup within the courtyard.
- Mechanical or electrical rooms should not be located within or overlooking any courtyard which has noise-sensitive rooms located around it.

Rain noise should be controlled so that it does not increase the target ambient noise level within any space by 20 dB. Guidelines on roof specifications are given in Chapter 4.

External mechanical rooms such as rooftop equipment associated with the building should be located away from patient treatment areas. It is often advisable to spread the location of rooftop equipment across the roof rather than gathered in a single location, to avoid noise buildup. Locating rooftop equipment areas towards façades where existing noise levels are higher (e.g., those overlooking a road) can help to mask the overall noise buildup. An allowance in rooftop equipment design should be made for the inclusion of an acoustic barrier, such as a louvered acoustic screen or solid barrier with an absorptive internal face. Guidelines on such screens are given in Chapter 4.

8.3.2 Room adjacencies to avoid

The room adjacencies detailed in Table 8.2 should be avoided.

Table 8.2 **Room adjacencies to avoid**

Room	Room
Operating rooms	Main kitchen/delivery rooms/nurseries
Nurseries	Archive rooms/lecture theaters/chapel/ multisensory rooms/speech therapy/ operating rooms
Delivery rooms	Archive rooms/lecture theaters/chapel/ multisensory rooms/speech therapy
Multisensory rooms/speech therapy rooms	Main kitchen/nurseries/delivery rooms
Chapel	Main kitchen/nurseries/delivery rooms
Main kitchen	Archive rooms/lecture theaters/ operating rooms/multi-sensory rooms/ speech therapy rooms/chapel

Note: Placing patient treatment or consultation rooms below either heavily trafficked areas (e.g., corridors) or physiotherapy gyms should be avoided.

8.3.3 Room layout

The following guidelines on planning and room massing are suggested:

■ Group service activities, such as laundries, main kitchens, main stores and mechanical rooms, together so that they can be located away from noise-sensitive space (treatment/consultation rooms, etc.). This will help reducing noise impact from the activities within these rooms, as well as noise associated with mail deliveries and waste disposal.

■ Avoid placing noise-sensitive rooms so that they have a direct view of any primary service areas (e.g., waste stores, loading bays).

■ Locate imaging equipment (e.g., MRI) at ground-floor level and away from noise-sensitive locations. This will help reduce any impact from noise and vibration from such equipment, while also reducing any potential interference from unwanted vibration from external sources.

■ Operating rooms should be positioned in a quiet part of the building away from any heavy traffic areas. Sudden high noise events should be controlled as far as it is practical.

■ Allowing for a separate mechanical building to accommodate HVAC units can significantly reduce mechanical noise issues.

■ Including smaller, multiple nurses' stations rather than large nurses' stations can help reduce noise buildup around hospital wards and treatment areas.

■ Include buffer zones between waiting areas and treatment/consultation rooms. Bathroom facilities, as well as doors, between waiting areas and corridors to treatment rooms are possible solutions.

■ Avoid placing treatment or consultation rooms directly off main circulation routes or in close proximity to café/dining spaces.

■ Where possible, the provision of single bed wards should be encouraged over multi-bed wards, as they have been found to reduce recovery times for patients.

■ For large or medium-sized wards as well as admittance areas (e.g., emergency rooms) include small meeting rooms to allow for confidential discussion between patients, visitors, and medical staff.

■ Service and passenger lifts/elevators should be located well away from any noise-sensitive room. They will also have to be separated from any vibration-sensitive laboratory or medical equipment.

8.3.4 Room design

■ Avoid the use of interconnecting doors between treatment/consultation rooms. Entrance doors to consulting or treatment rooms should be located as far apart as possible. Glazed panels to the side of a door but within the doorframe are likely to reduce the overall performance of a partition and should only be included for operational reasons.

■ Screen off areas within wards or nurses' stations which are used for preparing medication or completing patient charts. Three-sided booths can be useful, as they can provide some screening as well as clearly defining an area where tasks requiring high levels of concentration are undertaken.

■ Allow for the provision of secluded or withdrawn areas off corridors or wards. This allows for visitors to find informal spaces to hold semi-private discussions or congregate prior to, or after, visiting periods without causing significant disturbance to patients.

- It is generally recommended that partitions are taken up to the underside of the structural floor soffit with any suspended ceiling stopped by the room walls. This is of particular importance in noise-sensitive rooms or rooms where confidential discussions take place.

- The use of positive air pressure rooms in intensive care units can be useful in controlling the spread of infection as well as separating potential noisy observation areas from patients.

8.3.5 Sound masking

The principles of sound masking are discussed in Chapter 3. Sound masking can be a useful way of covering noise which patients and staff may find disturbing, and it is often worth considering for very quiet sites. Sound masking has been used successfully in the following types of spaces:

- mental health wards or social interaction spaces in residential care facilities
- any space where there are multiple treatment cubicles (e.g. curtains)
- large to medium-sized office space
- waiting areas
- large to medium-sized wards
- treatment/examination rooms
- spaces close to delivering or maternity rooms.

Masking levels of L_{Aeq} 48 dB are generally accepted as reasonable during daytime periods. For wards or areas where sleeping may occur this level will have to be adjusted for nighttime periods. This will depend on the underlying noise level on site but reductions of 10 dB between daytime and nighttime are expected to be reasonable. Active masking systems are available which adjust to the ambient noise level within the room as it changes.

Note: the inclusion of an effective noise masking system may allow for the acoustic performance of separating partitions to be reduced by 5 dB. This would not apply to delivery or maternity rooms.

8.3.6 Ducted air services

Healthcare buildings are usually heavily serviced buildings requiring substantial design allowances for air conditioning equipment.

■ As outlined in Figure 7.4, where possible main service ducts should be run along corridors and enter rooms via the corridor wall. Running services directly through walls which separate noise-sensitive rooms should be avoided.

■ It is anticipated that any Mechanical and Electrical (M&E) contractor will be expected to provide mechanical equipment which does not give rise to noise levels which exceed the guidance on noise levels given in Appendix B.

■ The use of an acoustically attenuating ceiling tile should be considered in any design (e.g., ceilings with a minimum rating of CAC 35 or $D_{n,c,w}$ 35 dB).

■ Cross-talk attenuators should be allowed for in ducts which service two or more rooms. These normally take the form of attenuators placed within the duct or flexible lined duct sections.

■ Introducing bends in a duct system can help reduce noise breakout at the grill. *Note*: bends in duct systems can lead to noise breakout levels increasing at other locations, and so wrapping the duct in a mass layer with an absorptive lining should also be considered. Additional bends may also require higher levels of air pressure through an AC system.

■ Standard duct attenuation methods are often not feasible in healthcare buildings due to clinical requirements. The use of bagged/sealed absorptive materials or non-fibrous materials may need to be considered or allowances may need to be made for significant space provision for fresh air plenums to ducting systems (i.e., large boxes located prior to duct terminations which help reduce air noise through a ventilation system).

■ Air transfer grills at duct system terminations should be selected on their acoustic performance.

8.3.7 Electrical, gas and water services

■ The use of flashing light alarms rather than audible alarms is preferable for emergency alarm systems in intensive care or infant care units. It is, however, expected that this will have to be cleared with any health and safety requirements.

■ Silent ringing telephones are also preferable in intensive care or infant care units.

■ Gas and air outlets along with electrical sockets and switches should ideally be mounted on service panels rather than being cored out of any separating partition. Placing such services back to back on either side of a partition should also be avoided.

■ Waste and water pipes for wash handbasins and bathrooms should be run through separate service ducts and not run within separating partitions or recessed into separating partitions.

■ Heating pipes and water pipes should be fitted with resilient mounts in areas where they are fixed to partitions within rooms used for sleeping.

8.3.8 Vibration and impact noise

The control of vibration is a complex subject and where necessary specialist advice should be sought. The nature of the equipment used in health care buildings often means that particular care should be taken when dealing with vibration sources. The following outlines general guidelines on this subject in relation to the control of structure-borne sound.

■ Full concrete constructions have been found to provide better inherent levels of vibration control than steel and concrete composite constructions.

■ Composite steel and concrete constructions can achieve good levels of vibration control but usually require the overall mass of the floor to be almost double that required for purely structural reasons.

■ It is unlikely that suitable levels of vibration can be achieved from lightweight timber floor structures without the inclusion of significant additional mass and isolation (e.g., concrete screeds and proprietorial isolation systems).

■ Table 8.3 outlines suitable vibration control levels for a range of room types. These levels do not guarantee complete control of vibration particularly for specialist medical and laboratory equipment. The guidelines given in the table allow for average performance levels but should be seen as performance levels for any individual event rather than an average for hypersensitive areas such as operating rooms and specialist laboratories.

■ Irregularities in floor surface (e.g., threshold bars and expansion joints) should be minimized or located in low traffic areas to reduce noise from trolleys and wheeled beds.

■ Rubberized flooring, resilient underlay, or backing for vinyl flooring can help to reduce footfall noise as well as limit vibration from trolleys and

Table 8.3 **Suggested vibration control levels (adapted from Cavanaugh et al. 2006 and Concrete Centre, 2004)**

Room	Acceleration ($_{RMS\,1\,sec}$) (W_g Frequency Weighting)	Vibration peak velocity (micro-in/s)
Wards	0.2ms–1.75	2000
Treatment areas	0.4ms–0.75	4000
Offices/consultation	0.8ms–1.75	8000

wheeled beds. (*Note*: Resilient underlay or backings can be prone to puncture so care should be taken when specifying.)

8.3.9 Clinical requirements and room finishes

The following recommendations are given:

- In clinical areas, the use of cleanable absorptive ceilings is desirable. Ceiling tiles that can be pressure- or steam-washed, and/or wall panels with an impermeable layer such as a vinyl finish, are preferable.
- The use of ceiling systems which include anti-microbial films on their exposed surfaces is advisable for clinical areas.
- Ceiling- or wall-mount absorptive finishes which include any horizontal surface which could allow for dust or dirt to gather should be avoided. Fix wall-mounted panels hard against the joint between the wall and the ceiling to avoid the creation of a horizontal surface.
- Avoid suspended ceiling grids in mental healthcare units in favor of perforated plasterboard ceilings or surface-mounted absorptive tiles/panels.
- The use of standard acoustically absorptive materials in non-clinical areas is normally permissible. For spaces such as atria, it is likely that the same approach as that outlined for school atria can be adopted.
- Consider including additional absorption in noise-sensitive areas within larger spaces, e.g., nurses' stations or areas where medicine is prepared or medical charts are filled in.

8.3.10 Separating partitions

Specification details for good practice when constructing separating walls and floors are given in the drawings in Appendix C.

Note: Where it is not possible to meet the minimum acoustic absorption requirements (set out in Table 8.4), then the level of insulation for the partitions in these areas should be increased by 3 dB.

8.3.11 Room finishes

Table 8.4 outlines suggested wall, floor, and ceiling finishes to ensure the control of reverberation and good speech intelligibility within a variety of healthcare type rooms, α_w are given for ceiling and wall panel finishes. Suitable material types may be limited due to clinical requirements. Appendix C includes possible finishes.

Table 8.4 Recommended floor, wall, and ceiling finishes by material or absorption coefficient α_w (healthcare)

Room description	Floor α_w	Ceiling finish α_w	Wall α_w
Clinical spaces			
Ward (single/ multi-person)	Unrated cleanable finish	0.65–0.8 over full ceiling (allowance for lighting)	Unrated cleanable finish
Mental healthcare/ long-term care	Unrated cleanable finish	0.65 over full ceiling assumed perforated plasterboard or bonded tiles	Unrated cleanable finish
Medical treatment (operating theaters/ MRI/ultrasound)	Unrated cleanable finish	0.65–0.95 over full ceiling (allowance for lighting); lower performance specification permissible if clinical requirements dictate	Unrated cleanable finish
Intensive care/ recover room (ICU/infant care)	Unrated cleanable finish	0.85–0.9 over full ceiling (allowance for lighting)	Unrated cleanable finish
Consultation rooms	Unrated cleanable finish	0.9 over full ceiling (allowance for lighting)	Unrated cleanable finish
Non-clinical areas			
Changing rooms	Vinyl flooring unrated	0.8 over full ceiling area (allowance for lighting)	Plaster or tile

Table 8.4 continued

Room description	Floor α_w	Ceiling finish α_w	Wall α_w
Corridors/stairwells	Vinyl flooring unrated	0.9 over full ceiling area (allowance for lighting)	Plaster or painted brick/block
Kitchens	Vinyl/tile unrated	0.8 over full ceiling area	Plaster or tile
Lecture room large >50 students	0.3 Carpet	0.8 over rear 75 percent of ceiling	0.8 over 25 percent of wall distributed over the back wall and the rear of the side walls
Lecture room small	< 50 students	0.3 Carpet	0.8 over 50 percent of ceiling 0.8 over 25 percent of walls located to rear of room
Record rooms	0.3 Carpet	0.9 over full ceiling (allowance for lighting)	Plaster finish
Meeting rooms	0.3 Carpet	0.8 over 50 percent of ceiling	0.8 over 25 percent of wall area
Laboratories	Vinyl unrated	0.8 over full ceiling (allowance for lighting)	Plaster/painted block finish
Toilets/showers	Vinyl flooring unrated	0.8 over full ceiling (allowance for lighting)	Plaster or tile

Further reading

Anjali, J., and Ulrich, R. (2007) *Sound control for improved outcomes in healthcare settings.* Concord, CA: Centre for Health Care Design.

Cavanaugh, W. J., et al. (2006) *Draft interim sound and vibration design guidelines for hospitals and healthcare facilities.* Acoustical Society of America/Institute of Noise Control Engineering/National Council of Acoustical Consultants.

Ceilings and Interior Systems Construction Association (CISCA) (2010) *Acoustics in healthcare Environments.* Oak Brook, IL: CISCA.

Concrete Centre (2004) *Hospital floor vibration study. Comparison of possible hospital floor structures with respect to NHS vibration criteria.* London: Ove Arup & Partners.

Department of Health (2013) *Specialist services – health technical memorandum, 08-01: Acoustics.* London: Department of Health.

James, A., and Zoontjens, L. (2012) Helicopter noise impacts on hospital development design. *Proceedings of Acoustics* 2012, November 21–23, Fremantle, Australia, Australian Acoustical Society.

Maynard, R., and Moorhouse, A. (2009) *Environmental noise and health in the UK.* London: Health Protection Agency/Public Health England.

chapter 9

Offices

9.1 The importance of good acoustics in office design

THE IMPORTANCE OF GOOD ACOUSTICS within offices and its link to worker productivity has been known since the 1940s. It can take up to 30 minutes for a person to regain full concentration on a task after being interrupted (DeMarco & Lister 1987) and 50 percent of office workers surveyed indicated that noise stops them from being as productive as possible (GSA, 2011).

Loss of productivity is not the only issue that should concern the architect or designer. The other key acoustic issue in offices is the provision of confidentiality. Whether it is for the meeting rooms of a corporate law firm or simply a small meeting room where difficult discussions occur, confidentiality is a key requirement for any office. Therefore the aim is to design spaces which allow for a balance between achieving good levels of confidentiality and reducing disturbance.

9.1.1 Disturbance vs. confidentiality

If we attempt to control noise disturbance, particularly from external and fixed mechanical sources producing too low a level, we run the risk of creating an environment in which activity within the office becomes more disturbing and where providing confidentiality is increasingly difficult to achieve.

Figure 6.2 should be referred to when considering the balance between controlling ambient noise, i.e., the level of steady noise such as external traffic and the level of acoustic insulation provided by separating partitions. If the background noise level is decreased, the insulation value of the partition must be increased to avoid the possibility of speech in an adjoining room being understood and/or heard. If the insulation value of the partition is low, then higher non-intrusive ambient noise levels would be required to mask speech from an adjoining room.

It is possible to adjust the performance of a separating wall by increasing the wall's acoustic performance and also controlling flanking transmission.

To adjust the effects of ambient noise, we can:

- alter the level of noise break-in from outside
- control noise from fixed mechanical equipment and machinery associated with the building
- reduce or increase the level of reverberation within a room
- introduce masking noise to cover disruptive ambient sound or create more non-disruptive ambient sound

This chapter aims to provide guidance on achieving speech privacy and reducing disturbance for the office worker.

9.2 Performance criteria

9.2.1 Performance specifications

Appendix B details suitable ambient noise levels, suitable control levels for fixed mechanical equipment, and suggested maximum reverberation times for each space. It should be noted that for many spaces a range is given for ambient and NC/NR (Noise Criterion, US; Noise Rating, UK) levels. The aim is not to create an entirely silent space but to allow for the inclusion of some non-intrusive steady noise, which can help to act as a masking source for more disturbing noises (e.g. loud speech, sudden sounds, etc.).

9.2.2 Sound insulation between spaces

Airborne sound insulation performance and impact sound insulation performance levels for offices are also given in Tables 8.3 and B.1 respectively). Requirements may differ depending upon the core activity within the office or the building type with which it is associated.

9.2.3 Control of speech noise in open-plan and large spaces

The speech transmission index, as detailed in Chapter 5, provides a performance target within a space, rather than between spaces, and in particular in open-plan or very large office spaces. The nature of the space will dictate the relevance of the speech transmission index (STI). For example, in open-plan

Table 9.1 Recommended speech transmission indices by open-plan or large room type-speech overheard between workstations or listeners (Irish, 2012)

STI	Subjective intelligibility	Subjective privacy	Suitable room type
0–0.3	Bad	Good	Call center
0.3–0.45	Poor	Reasonable	Call center
0.45–0.6	Fair	Poor	Interactive open-plan office
0.6–0.75	Good	Very poor	Seminar room Board room

call centers the aim would be for a low STI, in order to reduce the disturbance of a conversation by one operator affecting another operator. Conversely, for rooms where training activities take place it is preferable to have a high STI so occupants can clearly understand the spoken word. Table 9.1 outlines the subjective STI levels and references them with some suitable room types.

Normal speech from one person at 3 ft (1 m) would be around L_{Aeq} 57 dB, while raised speech would be around L_{Aeq} 65 dB. Within open-plan offices, speech disturbance can be controlled to a reasonable standard where the noise level from speech reduces to below L_{Aeq} 48 dB at a distance of 13 ft (4 m). This distance can be reduced when the workers face away from each other. Therefore

- ■ Two workers face-to-face, 13 ft (4 m) apart, normal speaking: <48 dB criteria achieved.
- ■ Two workers back-to-back, 6 ft (2 m) apart, normal speaking: <48 dB criteria achieved.

At closer distances, or with higher speech levels, additional treatments would be required, e.g., barriers or noise masking.

9.2.4 Noise from maximum noise events, rain noise, and lift/elevator noise

The ambient noise criteria given in Appendix B provide indicative standards for anonymous noise break-in and adequate control levels for most office room types. With regards to maximum noise levels from sudden or impulsive

Table 9.2 Control levels for various noise sources – offices

Room	External sources	Rain noise	Lift/elevator noise
	$L_{Amax(f)}$ dB	NR/NC	$L_{Amax(f)}$ dB
Open-plan office	55	50	55
Meeting room	45	45	30
Reception	55	50	50
Small office	50	45	40

external noise sources or noise from rain or lift/elevators, guidelines are given in Table 9.2.

In instances where there is a preference for natural ventilation, the L_{Aeq} and L_{Amax} levels for external sources should be relaxed by +5 dB.

9.2.5 Internal doors and openings

Table 9.3 suggests insulation levels for office doors and links them to possible door types and room locations.

Table 9.3 Suggested door specifications

Door type	Expected performance rating STC/R_w dB	Suitable location
Glazed door no gasket or frameless 6–8 mm glass	25–28	Reception area, informal meeting, storage, open-plan office
Glazed door with frame and/or gasket 6–8 mm glass	28–30	Reception area, informal meeting, withdrawn workspace, open-plan office
Timber/metal door (light 4 4mm @ 27 kg/m²)	30	Withdrawn working, small offices, toilets, staff rooms
Timber/metal door (heavy 54 mm @ 29 kg/m²)	35	Seminar rooms, confidential meeting rooms, mechanical and server rooms

9.2.6 Flanking via glazing mullions

Sound transmission via external glazing elements between office spaces is possible. With regards to horizontal transmission, mullion specification should be set as follows:

- group office space to group offices spaces: min $D_{nE,n}$ 45 dB
- group to withdrawn or private office space: min $D_{nE,n}$ 53 dB
- withdrawn /private office to withdrawn/private office: min $D_{nE,n}$ 53 dB.

The basic performance requirement can usually be achieved with the inclusion of an expanding spray foam or foam pad within a boxed mullion. The enhanced performance requirement can usually be achieved with the inclusion of two foam pads separated by a 100 mm gap within the boxed mullion.

9.2.7 Noise masking

It is often necessary to introduce background noise into an office space to improve speech privacy and reduce disturbance, particularly within open-plan offices. Electronic noise-masking systems can be used to help achieve required continuous, unobtrusive background noise levels that mask or cover intrusive sound.

Open-plan spaces: masking levels of between L_{Aeq} 45–48 dB are considered optimal.

Enclosed spaces: masking levels of between L_{Aeq} 38–42 dB are considered optimal.

9.3 Design guidelines

9.3.1 Controlling external noise

For naturally ventilated offices, the control of external noise will be dictated by the standoff distance to the noise source. For busy roads minimum standoff distances of 328 ft (100 m) can be effective. To reduce standoff distances, the application of mitigation such as barriers and attenuated ventilation would be necessary (see comment in Chapter 4). The following advice is recommended:

■ Orient buildings so that you minimize the length of building façade exposed to a major noise source, e.g., road, industrial plant.

■ Try to adopt floor layouts that place ancillary space and non-noise-sensitive rooms along the façade most exposed to noise.

■ Consider placing noise critical spaces, e.g., video conferencing rooms within central core areas.

■ Consider layouts with central courtyards, to provide optimum natural light and ventilation while limiting external noise exposure.

■ Place office space that can tolerate higher internal ambient levels along façades that are exposed to greater continuous ambient noise (e.g. road noise).

9.3.2 Control of internal noise

Figure 9.1 offers a design consideration diagram to help in the selection of room relationships during initial client discussions. It is important to understand what activities are likely to be undertaken within each office development and the required floor area for each activity. By grouping activities by noise characteristics and sound requirements usability, issues can be avoided.

1) Place private meeting spaces and board room along a separate corridor, for additional privacy and to allow for pre- and post-meeting discussions to take place away from areas where it may cause disturbance.

2) Cluster ancillary activities together, to limit the need for enhanced acoustic insulation between spaces and also to separate potentially disturbing noise (e.g., lift/elevator noise) away from working areas.

3) Avoid placing doors to private office space on both sides of the separating partition between any two rooms.

4) Cluster private office space and small withdrawn working spaces together.

5) Place informal meeting spaces away from work requiring high levels of concentration.

6) Cluster high-interaction workstations together to simplify specification of finishes.

7) Small meeting spaces are useful in providing space for semi-confidential discussions, activities requiring sporadic withdrawn working, or prolonged telephone conversations. Such spaces should be easily accessible to encourage use. They can also be used as a buffer between areas.

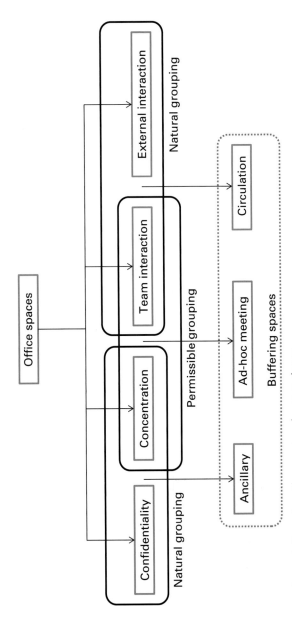

9.1 Suggested office outline with comments on the acoustic features

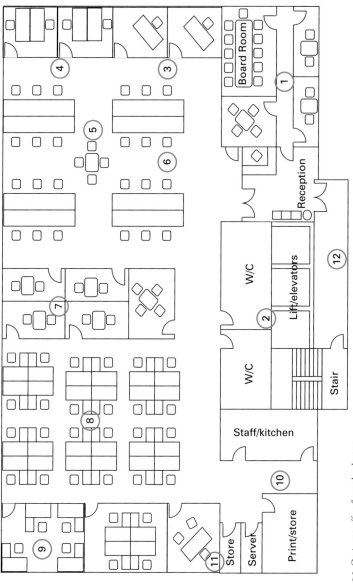

9.2 Optimum office floor-plan layout

8) Cluster together those work activities requiring concentration or withdrawn working.

9) Tasks requiring prolonged concentration and withdrawn working are better suited to small offices. Desk location can also be key: workers facing each other is preferable for frequent interaction, workers facing away from each other will improve privacy and reduce disturbance.

10) Locate staff services away from the main office area, to reduce possible disturbance.

11) Use storage areas to provide noise buffers between high noise areas and quiet spaces.

12) Placing ancillary areas along the façade which has the highest exposure to noise can reduce disturbance to the remaining office space.

(see Figures 9.1 and 9.2 on pages 144 and 145)

Figure 9.3 offers guidance on the control of noise within open-plan office areas.

1) Positioning absorptive clouds above informal meeting areas can help to improve speech privacy. A minimum absorption coefficient of α_w 0.8 is suggested.

2) Introducing areas where the ceiling height drops between groups or along circulation areas can reduce sound transmission around the space.

3) Floor-to-ceiling heights should not exceed 11.5 ft (3.5 m). Acoustically absorptive ceiling are preferable, with a minimum absorption coefficient of α_w 0.9.

4) Acoustically absorptive dividers should not exceed a height of 3 ft (90 cm) from ground level. Allowing for some eye contact increases worker awareness of fellow workers and reduces prevalence for loud speech that may occur when a sense of privacy is offered by divider panels.

5) Use of carpets or carpet tiles is preferred, as this will help reducing noise buildup from footfall and chair movement noise. It will also reduce impact sound transmission to lower rooms. Finishes with a minimum ΔL_w of 21 dB are preferable.

6) Placing acoustically absorptive panels on walls will help reducing room reverberation. For both wall panels and freestanding panels, a minimum absorption coefficient of α_w 0.8 is suggested.

7) Freestanding acoustic divider panels between workstations should be as

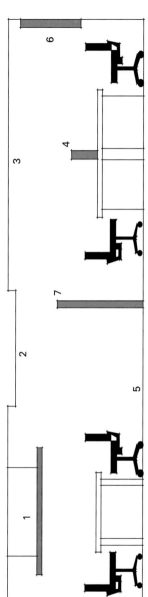

9.3 Section through an open-plan office (adapted from BSI, 2004)

close to the workstation as possible, not placed halfway between two workstations. Glazed or Perspex vision panels should be considered for panels which are above 3 ft (90 cm) in height. Barrier effects from divider panels will be improved if they form a continuous barrier around a workstation and gaps around freestanding panels are avoided.

(see Figure 9.3, page 147)

Suggested design consideration for reception areas are:

- ■ Place a low acoustically absorptive ceiling and/or acoustically absorptive wall linings around the reception desk.
- ■ Locate the reception desk away from intrusive noise sources, e.g., vending machines, foyer cafés, lifts, mechanical equipment.
- ■ Separate reception desks from seating areas so receptionists can talk on the phone without being understood by visitors, while visitors can talk quietly amongst themselves without being overheard. Separating distances of 13 ft (4 m) or greater are optimal. Distances of more than 32 ft (10 m) should be avoided so that the receptionist can still attract a visitor's attention.
- ■ Discourage waiting next to the reception desk, to reduce disturbance for other guests or when telephone calls are being taken. Place company literature/visual displays or focal points away from the reception desk.
- ■ Introduce background noise to help create privacy if reception areas are found to be too quiet, i.e., an active noise masking system.
- ■ Do not place small meeting rooms and offices, with glazed walls and doors, directly off of a reception area. This can be problematic where confidentiality is a major concern.

9.4 Guidelines on specification

9.4.1 Avoiding risk

Figure 9.4 shows the normal location for electrical service tracking and floor through ventilation/heating – both common details in office developments. Where electrical cabling is run through the wall, there is a requirement for any gaps around the cabling to be filled with either a gypsum-based caulk or with an adjustable fire seal sleeve.

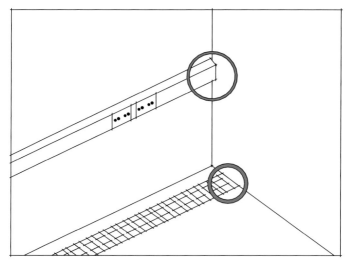

9.4 Electrical and ventilation/heating detail

Where floor or ceiling through ventilation/heating is taken under a separating wall, it is necessary to include a cross-talk attenuator on either side of the partition. Attenuators which are between 19 in (500 mm) and 39 in (1000 mm) should be detailed for either side of the partition.

Note: Where privacy is of paramount importance, such details should be avoided.

The following recommendations should also be considered:

- Use surface-mounted electrical and computer sockets rather than cutting the plasterboard on office walls.
- Run mechanical and electrical services along corridors; avoid running services over the top of walls that separate acoustically sensitive rooms.
- Avoid running suspended ceiling grids over the top of partitions designed for acoustically sensitive rooms. Even with acoustic baffle, details above ceiling grids can allow for some sound transmission.
- Avoid the use of glazed partitions or partially glazed partitions for walls that separate rooms where privacy is important.
- Incorporate framed doors, glazed or solid core, in the design of rooms where privacy is important.

■ Avoid the inclusion of demountable partitions in the design of boardrooms, executive offices, private working offices, and private meeting rooms.

9.4.2 Room finishes

Table 9.4 outlines suggested wall, floor, and ceiling finishes to ensure the control of reverberation and good speech intelligibility within a range of office accommodations, α_w are given for ceiling and wall panel finishes. Examples of suitable materials would be mineral fiber ceiling tiles, fabric-covered foam or fiber-backed panels or perforated timber veneer acoustic panels (see Appendix C for a list of suitable finishes).

Table 9.4 Recommended floor, wall, and ceiling finishes by material or absorption coefficient ἀw (offices)

Room	Floor α_w	Ceiling finish α_w	Wall α_w
Reception	0.3 Carpet or hard surface (unrated)	0.8 over full ceiling, consider absorptive cloud over reception desk	0.8 over 25 percent of wall area
Cafeteria	0.3 Carpet or hard surface (unrated)	0.8 over full ceiling	0.8 over 25 percent of wall area
Single/executive office	0.3 Carpet	0.8 over full ceiling	Plaster finish
Confidential/ interview meeting room	0.3 Carpet	0.8 over 50 percent of ceiling	0.8 over 25 percent of wall area
Board room	0.3 Carpet	0.8 over 50 percent of ceiling	0.8 over 25 percent of wall area
Small office 2–8 people	0.3 Carpet	0.8 over full ceiling	0.05 plaster finish
Large office >8–15 people	0.3 Carpet	0.9 over full ceiling	0.05 plaster finish
Open-plan quiet working	0.3 Carpet	0.9 over full ceiling	See comment regarding absorptive screens
Open-plan interactive working	0.3 Carpet	0.8 over full ceiling	See comment regarding absorptive screens

Room	Floor α_w	Ceiling finish α_w	Wall α_w
Small meeting <5 people	0.3 Carpet	0.8 over 50 percent of ceiling	0.8 over 25 percent of wall area
Large meeting > 5–20 people	0.3 Carpet	0.8 over 50 percent of ceiling	0.8 over 25 percent of wall area
Informal meeting/ telephone room	0.3 Carpet	0.8 over 50 percent of ceiling	0.8 over 25 percent of wall area
Seminar room	0.3 Carpet	0.9 over full ceiling	0.8 over 25 percent of wall located to rear of room
Tele/ videoconferencing room	0.3 Carpet	0.9 over full ceiling	0.8 over 25 percent of wall area
Lecture room <50 people	0.3 Carpet	0.8 over 50 percent of ceiling	0.8 over 25 percent of wall located to rear of room
Lecture room >50 people	0.3 Carpet	0.8 over rear 75 percent of ceiling	0.8 over 25 percent of wall located to rear of room
Staff room/ staff kitchen	0.3 Carpet or hard surface (unrated)	0.5–0.7 over full ceiling	0.05 plaster finish
Bathroom/ changing room	0.3 Carpet or hard surface (unrated)	0.5–0.7 over full ceiling	0.05 plaster finish
Computer server room	0.3 Carpet or hard surface (unrated)	0.8 over full ceiling	0.05 plaster finish
Mechanical room	0.3 Carpet or hard surface (unrated)	0.8 over full ceiling	0.05 plaster finish

Suitable separating partition details are outlined in Appendix C.

Further reading

British Standards Institution (BSI) (2004) *Acoustics, guidelines for noise control in office and workrooms by means of acoustical screens.* BS EN ISO 17624. London: BSI.
British Council for Offices (BCO) (2009) *Guide to specification.* London: BCO.

DeMarco, T., and Lister T. (1987) *Peopleware, productivity projects and teams.* London: Addison Wesley.

General Services Administration (GSA) (2011) *Sound matters – How to achieve acoustic comfort in the contemporary office.* Washington, DC: GSA Public Buildings Services.

Central Computer and Telecommunications Agency (CCAT) (1994) *Management of acoustic noise* (IT infrastructure Library). London: HMSO.

Irish, M. (2012) Acoustic design assessment, office development. Unpublished technical report, RMP Acoustics, Edinburgh.

Shield, B. (2009) *Review of research on office acoustics, a report for the Association of Interior Specialists.* London: AIS.

Veitch, J. A., and Naevia, M. (2003) *Acoustic satisfaction in open plan offices: Review and recommendations.* Ottawa: NRC-CNRC.

chapter 10

Theaters/Auditoriums

10.1 The importance of good acoustics in theaters and auditoriums

THEATERS AND AUDITORIUMS are intended for performances and events where speech is the most important signal of interest. For this reason, speech intelligibility is the single most important acoustic parameter to consider. There are entire textbooks devoted to this type of venue and we don't pretend to get too deep into the details, but will give you a general overview and recommendations that will serve to inform the design process.

Theaters and auditoriums often use amplified sound but, since it is not the purpose of this text to discuss sound system design, we will discuss how to make the best passive acoustic decisions when designing this type of venue.

Amplified sound will aid in the intelligibility of speech, and this can be enhanced with architectural elements. However, too many reflective surfaces will inevitably end in higher reverberation times that will have a detrimental effect on speech intelligibility, so the process to design good acoustics for a theater is a careful balance between absorptive surfaces and carefully placed sound reflectors.

10.2 Performance criteria

10.2.1 Reverberation times

Reverberation times in a theater need to be short enough to protect speech intelligibility. Figure 10.1 presents some optimum reverberation times for speech relative to room volumes and use of the space. It is not the intention to have a very dry space, since this type of venue will usually have music as a secondary activity (e.g., opera or musical theater, where speech intelligibility is the priority, but music quality is also desirable).

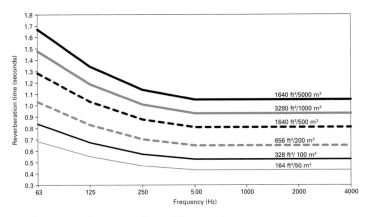

10.1 Optimum reverberation times for speech by room volume

10.2.2 Clarity, C50

Speech clarity (C50) is a measure of the ratio between early and late energy. This means that it gives an idea of how the balance is between the helpful early reflections and the late reverberation. It is called C50 because it defines the limit between early and late reflections as 50 ms, which, as discussed in Chapter 3, is the point at which our brain starts being able to separate individual reflections.

$$C50 = \frac{Energy\ before\ 50\ ms}{Energy\ after\ 50\ ms}\ ,\ in\ dB$$

The higher the value for C50, the more clarity, and so the better speech intelligibility the room will have. In Eq. A.26 (in Appendix A) we explain how to calculate C50.

Definition, (D) There is a similar parameter that is used in the acoustic analysis of auditoriums and it is called definition (D). It is the ratio between the energy arriving during the first 50 ms and the total energy:

$$D = \frac{Energy\ before\ 50\ ms}{Total\ energy}\ ,\ in\ dB$$

10.3 Design guidelines

10.3.1 Recommended room volumes

Table 10.1 outlines suitable room volumes for a variety of occupations and uses. These are spaces where listening is a key requirement, such as musical recitals or theater performances. The levels use the number of audience members (or people intended to use the room) as a guideline of required room volumes.

10.3.2 Distance from sound source to listener

Close proximity between a speaker or musical source and a listener is likely to mean that the sound can be easily heard, understood, and appreciated. Assuming other acoustic issues such as noise break-in and reverberation have been correctly treated, then the rule of thumb in Table 10.2 should hold true.

Rooms where the minimum distance between a speaker and listener exceeds 98 ft (30 m) are likely to result in some occupants having significant difficulty in hearing and understanding an unamplified voice. Therefore, a loudspeaker system may be necessary.

Table 10.1 **Suggested optimum volumes for good acoustics by room type**

Room type	Suggested volumes	
	ft³	m³
Lecture room	13–19 per seat	4–6 per seat
Theater	13–19 per seat	4–7 per seat
Multipurpose (speech/music)	19–29 per seat	6–9 per seat
Church	>33 per seat	>10 per seat

Table 10.2 **Maximum audience distance according to room use**

Room use	Maximum audience distance (ft/m)
Unamplified speech (very good)	<49 ft/15 m
Unamplified speech (good)	49–65 ft/15–20 m
Drama theater	<26 ft/50 m
Opera/ballet/chamber music	<98 ft/30 m
Orchestral music	<131 ft/40 m

The maximum permissible distances for audiences for theater and musical performances, along with indicative suitable areas per spectator, would suggest upper limits on audience sizes to ensure the quality of the listening experiences. This assumes that noise break-in and reverberation have been suitable controlled. These limitations could be overcome with the introduction of sound amplification systems (e.g., microphone and loudspeaker systems).

The seating limit for unamplified performances should be:

- Theater/drama – 1300 seats
- Chamber music – 1200 seats
- Opera/Ballet – 2300 seats
- Orchestral music – 3000 seats.

10.3.3 Balconies

A common way to shorten the distance between the source and the listener is to add balconies. The addition of a balcony will create an obstacle for the reflection coming from the ceiling to reach the audience underneath it, and in some cases separate that space acoustically so that a second reverberation time can be perceived (see Section 6.3.1). The lack of reflections in this area can be beneficial for speech intelligibility as long as early reflections from a ceiling reflector close to the source as well as lateral reflections are arriving at this zone. A rule of thumb is that the balcony depth should not exceed 2.5 times its height.

10.3.4 General guidelines

Figure 10.2 outlines good practice guidelines for rooms to be used for lecture theaters, seminar rooms or conference venues where there is a fixed position for an unamplified person speaking to a room:

1) Ensure a clear line of sight between speaker and each audience member.
2) Reflective surfaces close behind the speaker position help to reinforce an unamplified voice. Parallel surfaces on either side can cause flutter echoes.
3) Reflective surfaces above and to the front of the room help to direct sound down to listener positions.
4) Suspended panels can help to reduce the effective room volume and so reduce reverberation. Services can then be placed above panels, allowing for easier access.

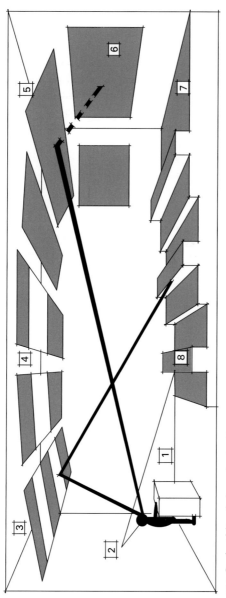

10.2 Good guidelines for lecture/seminar/theater space

5) Place acoustically absorptive materials towards the rear of the room, to avoid long delays between direct sound and reflected sound. Angle the last absorptive panel at the back of the hall so that it directs sound either down to the floor at the back of the room or onto the back wall.

6) Place acoustically absorptive panels on the back wall to absorb reflected sound from the roof, as well as to absorb direct sound from being reflected back into the space.

7) Carpeting floors can minimally reduce reverberation, but mainly reduces footfall and impact noise.

8) Acoustically absorptive upholstery on seating will help to ensure an even level of sound when the space is half full.

(see Figure 10.2, page 157)

Further reading

Egan, D. M. (1988) *Architectural Acoustics*. New York: McGraw-Hill, Inc.

Templeton, D., Sacre, P., Mapp, P. and Saunders, D. (1993) *Acoustics in the built environment: Advice for the design team*. London: Butterworth Architecture.

chapter 11

Concert halls

11.1 The importance of good acoustics in concert halls

CONCERT HALLS HAVE A VERY SPECIFIC acoustic intention: to provide the appropriate environment for good music quality. As opposed to theaters, concert halls do not put emphasis on speech intelligibility because their main purpose is musical performance. However, there is a wide range of music genres requiring different acoustic characteristics. There is, for example, Gregorian music and the qualities of the space necessary for that type of music are on one end of the music-genre scale (long reverberation times = live big rooms). On the other end we can find contemporary music (i.e., rock) with music qualities that have very different requirements (short reverberation times, amplification = dry/dead rooms). This chapter intends to give general guidelines regarding the design of spaces for music performance, without getting down to the details that are specific to the music genres.

11.2 Performance criteria

11.2.1 Reverberation time

Reverberation times for concert halls include a wide range of activities. Figure 11.1 provides a good guideline. In general, longer reverberation times are desired than for speech-based spaces, because musical notes in a composition do not need to be strictly separated to be understood. In fact, it is desirable that there is a small overlap between the tones to aid the flow or mellowness of the musical piece. Reverberation also increases the sense of envelopment in a room, which improves the experience.

After defining the appropriate reverberation time for a venue, it is necessary to decide where to put the absorption. Construction materials tend to be reflective, so even for long reverberation times it is often necessary to

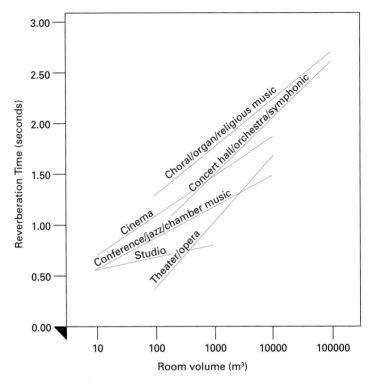

11.1 Optimum reverberation times for music venues

add absorptive materials. Furthermore, there are surfaces in a venue that you always want to cover with absorptive material simply to eliminate other acoustic issues (e.g., absorption in the back wall to avoid echoes).

Audience as the main absorber It is very common to find that the greatest area for absorption of sound in a venue is the audience area. Audiences will be absorbing when the area is fully occupied, mostly due to people's clothing. However, we cannot count on a venue always having a full house. For this reason we need to provide seating that resembles the acoustic properties of a full audience. Fully upholstered seats are a good choice; however, this is not always the design intent. In any case, calculating the amount of absorption that the audience at different levels of occupancy will provide is the first thing we need to consider before adding additional absorptive materials to the room surfaces. Variable acoustics can be considered to compensate for unoccupied seating designed to have very low absorption.

11.2.2 Clarity, C80

C80, or musical clarity is the equivalent of C50 from theaters. It defines a ratio between early energy (before 80 ms) and late energy (after 80 ms). Music clarity is measured with a limit of 80 ms as opposed to 50 ms for speech clarity, because, as mentioned before, music needs less separation of individual sounds, and this means some reverberation is accepted as a positive quality. For the calculation of C80, see Eq. A.27.

11.2.3 Subjective evaluation of concert halls

Particular terminology is often used to describe the perception of sound in concert halls. In acoustic evaluation it is as important to use the ears as it is to use measurement instruments.

For reverberation, it is common to say a room is dry/dead or live: Rooms which are acoustically dry tend to have short reverberation times, whereas rooms which are acoustically live tend to have long reverberation times. Acoustically drier rooms are generally more suitable for speech activities, while rooms which are more acoustically live are favorable for unamplified orchestra, choral music, or pipe organ music.

For clarity, we classify rooms as clear or muddy/blurry: Rooms which are acoustically clear usually have well-controlled reverberation levels so that echoes do not interfere with the gaps or lulls between words or syllables. Muddy rooms can have long reverberation times, causing interference in intelligibility. Clarity is also affected by room volume and background noise levels.

11.3 Typologies

CONCERT HALLS HAVE EVOLVED TOGETHER WITH MUSIC and their shapes have changed many times, trying to adapt to the music of the time as well as the architectural typologies and interior design. Halls during the Renaissance, for example, had ample decorations on the walls, which created a rich texture that facilitates sound diffusion. While this is not always the desired acoustic quality, it does eliminate many acoustic defects (e.g., echoes and focalizations). Table 11.1 and Figure 11.2 explain the main characteristics of some common typologies.

Table 11.1 Concert hall typologies

Typology	Description	Advantages	Disadvantages
Fan shape	The narrow part of the fan is towards the stage	Good visuals from every point	Lack of early reflections in front and center audience
		Large capacity	Lack of spatial impression to the absent lateral reflections
Shoebox	Rectangular, relatively narrow	Good early reflections	Small balconies
		High sound envelopment and spatial impression	
		Bad visuals from the front sides.	
Reverse fan shape	The large part of the fan is towards the stage	Great early reflections	Bad visuals for a large part of the audience
		High spatial impression	
Fan shape and reverse fan shape, or hexagonal	The room begins narrow, widens toward the center and narrows to the back again	Good visuals	
		Good early reflections	
		Good spatial impression	
Horseshoe	Typically used for the Italian opera houses.	Large capacity	Poor early reflections
			Possible focalization if back wall is not treated

Typology	Description	Advantages	Disadvantages
Multiple hexagonal shapes	Positions the audience at two levels, creating side walls for the smaller hexagon	Great lateral reflections High spatial impression Good visuals	
Terraced	Audience is located in smaller sections terraced around three or four sides of the stage	Good early reflections Good spatial impression Great visuals High capacity	Poor stage acoustics

11.4 Variable acoustics

EVEN THOUGH IT IS USUALLY NOT RECOMMENDED to design a venue that needs to serve different purposes requiring different acoustic conditions, sometimes it becomes necessary to have the ability to modify a space acoustically.

There are several ways to do this. Since our intent is usually to modify the reverberation of the room, we can do this by either changing the absorption in the room or changing the volume.

11.4.1 Change in materials

To change the materials of a room in order to modify its reverberation time is probably the easier of the two methods. This is done by replacing reflecting surfaces with absorptive ones, or vice versa, or in some cases with diffusive areas as well, not to change the reverberation time of the room but instead the quality of sound. Recording studios need to do this constantly, as well as multipurpose auditoriums. The acoustic needs of a room for music are very different than those of a room for speech, but, as mentioned before, even different types of music require different characteristics. There are many ways to easily change the surface materials of a room, which usually involve turning a panel that has two sides of different materials or hiding/uncovering surfaces of different materials. The following are some examples of this method.

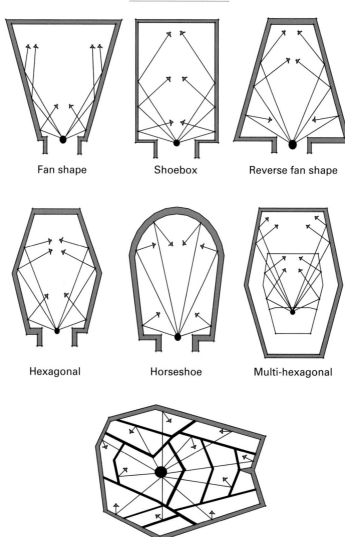

Fan shape Shoebox Reverse fan shape

Hexagonal Horseshoe Multi-hexagonal

Terraced

11.2 Concert hall typologies (see also Table 11.1)

Turning panels: In this case the absorptive panels are backed by a reflective surface and they are hinged to the wall, allowing them to be turned 180 degrees to expose the reflective side, while at the same time covering the fixed absorption of the wall (Figure 11.3).

Sliding panels: This example uses tracks to slide reflective panels over fixed absorption on the wall, or over fixed reflective panels to uncover either of them (Figure 11.4).

Perforated sliding panels: A wall covered with absorption material and a perforated plate is a composite absorber as explained in Section 2.5. An additional layer of perforated plate sliding over can either be lined up

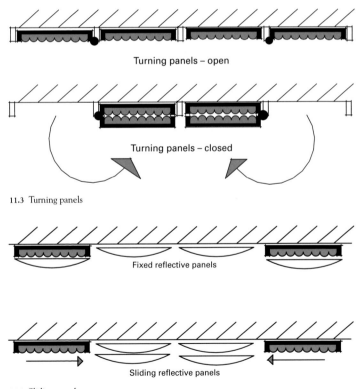

Turning panels – open

Turning panels – closed

11.3 Turning panels

Fixed reflective panels

Sliding reflective panels

11.4 Sliding panels

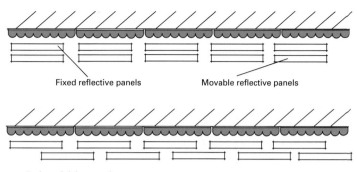

11.5 Perforated sliding panels

with the one behind to expose the openings, or unaligned to close them, creating only a reflective plate (Figure 11.5).

Turning prisms: Instead of a two-sided panel turning on a hinge, a prism can offer a third face to provide one more characteristic (e.g., scattering). The prisms would rotate on their center like those stripped billboards that change the picture by rotating to expose a different face.

Turning cylinders: Using the same mechanism as the turning prisms – but usually with only two materials, each covering half of the cylinder – is a way of varying between absorption and diffusion in the room. Commonly used in recording studios where a diffuse field is more desirable than strong specular reflections.

Curtains: A very simple way of replacing reflection with absorption in a wall is to draw heavy curtains to hide the reflective material.

Hanging panels: Another very simple way of replacing reflection with absorption is to hang an absorptive panel in a wall made of a reflective material, the same way you would hang a painting (Figure 11.6).

11.4.2 Change in volume

The second option for variable acoustics is to modify the volume of the room. This method is harder to achieve since it means changing the architecture of the room but it can also be achieved by several methods.

Dropping ceiling: A floating ceiling that is mechanically mounted to allow changing the position up and down, thus reducing the volume of the

11.6 Hanging panels in Troy Music Hall (Troy, NY)

room when less reverberation is desired (e.g., to change from orchestral music to opera). It can be composed by multiple elements like a ceiling cloud to facilitate the change.

Sliding wall: In some cases a performance with a requirement of a lower reverberation time can also be intended for a smaller audience. For example, a theatrical performance which requires less reverberation time than a music performance also requires the audience to be closer to the stage in order to appreciate the acting. A sliding wall that closes a section of the audience would significantly reduce the volume of the space but also its capacity. Sliding walls are commonly used in conference centers but they can also be used in traditional halls.

Coupled volumes: An additional volume connected or coupled to the main room can significantly vary its reverberation time or the perceived reverberation time, as sound which would have been reflected back into the space is allowed to propagate out into the coupled space and dissipate (see Section 2.1.1).

11.4.3 Electroacoustics

Lastly, an effective way to change reverberation time in a room is by means of electroacoustics. This method is only considered for amplified performances. Sound is captured by microphones on the performers and processed to augment reverberation before being sent back into the room. It is not possible to reduce reverberation time electronically, so a room designed for this method would be fairly dry.

11.5 Design guidelines

THE FOLLOWING GOOD PRACTICE GUIDELINES are for rooms to be used for orchestral music or any form of unamplified music.

■ Rectangular-shaped halls with high ceilings are normally preferable; fan-shaped halls normally provide poor acoustics for musical performances.

■ Domes and barrel vaults can cause focusing and should be avoided or treated with additional absorption (see Section 2.1.1).

■ Acoustic scattering treatments are useful. Side-wall diffusion can increase musical clarity.

- A proscenium stage enclosure will benefit the balance and ensemble of orchestrations.
- Large overhangs or balconies will reduce the quality of sound reaching those seated below.
- Shallow pitched roofs can cause flutter effects.
- Seating should be arranged to allow for a clear line of sight to the performance space for acoustic, as well as for visual reasons. This should help to ensure the same acoustics at each seat.
- Steeply inclined seating should be avoided, particularly for musical performance spaces.
- The walls, floor, and ceiling around the performance space should preferably be acoustically reflective. Acoustic absorption in these areas should be avoided.
- For music performance spaces, the acoustic absorption provided by unoccupied seating should be as similar as possible to when the seats are occupied. Upholstered seating is best. Where tip-up seating is used, it is preferable to upholster the underside of the seat.

11.5.1 Balconies

Balconies are used as a means of reducing the distance between the listener and performer. However, large balconies can become an obstacle for the reflections coming from the ceiling to reach the audience underneath it. To avoid this issue, balconies should not be too deep. A general rule of thumb for concert halls is that the balcony depth is not larger than its height. Multiple tiered balconies or shallow balconies on all sides of the audience (i.e., back and side balconies) are more desirable than one deep balcony. The addition of a balcony will also change the required room height as well as the volume/person, which will have an effect on reverberation and perception, so the addition of a balcony needs to come early in the design.

Further reading

Carrión Isbert, A. (2001) *Diseño acústico de espacios arquitectónics*. Madrid: Alfaomega S.L.

chapter 12

Dwellings

12.1 The importance of good acoustics in the design of homes

NEIGHBOR NOISE HAS ALWAYS BEEN CONSIDERED a significant factor in the rating of satisfaction in new and refurbished dwellings. The control of sound within dwellings is therefore a statutory requirement in most countries and it is also included in most assessment methods used to determine sustainability. In most instances the statutory requirements are set as minimum target values rather than optimum insulation levels and as a result there can be conflict between end-user expectation and national or regional requirements. The target values adopted around the world look to provide reasonable levels of insulation in the hope that this will satisfy the majority of occupants. For this reason, designers and developers should be wary of using terms like "soundproof," as even the best-performing walls and floor systems have the potential to allow for some transmission of sound.

12.2 Domestic sound insulation performance requirements

12.2.1 Partitions between dwellings

Table 12.1 details the level of occupant satisfaction compared to the measureable sound insulation for partitions separating dwellings. Appendix C outlines a limited number of partition types for use in separating constructions.

Controlling sound transmission is most important in adjoined dwellings and it is generally a requirement of building codes and regulations in many countries across the globe. Table 12.2 shows the expected performance levels required by different building regulations in some countries around the world.

Table 12.1 Perceived satisfaction levels of sound insulation for separating partitions (Smith et al., 2006)

Perceived rating	Airborne sound	Impact sound
	$D_{nT,w}$ (dB)	$L'_{nT,w}$ (dB)
A*Excellent	62–64	<47–49
A Very good	59–61	50–52
B Quite good	56–58	53–55
C Acceptable	53–55	56–58
D Barely acceptable	50–52	59–61
E Poor	47–49	62–64
F Very poor	44–46	65–67
G Intolerable	41–43	68–70>

12.2.2 Internal partitions

In addition to sound insulation between dwellings, it is considered good practice to ensure a minimum level of acoustic insulation for partitions within dwellings. Insulation levels of STC/R_w 40–43 dB should be seen as a minimum requirement for walls and floors within a house.

The use of single stud partitions with high-mass plasterboard linings (e.g., minimum 10 kg/m^2) and the inclusion of a layer of mineral fiber quilt would provide a minimum specification to achieve this level.

12.2.3 Doors to apartments/flats

Doors to apartments/flats which open onto a common lobby or stairwell should be specified as having a minimum performance of STC/R_w 29 dB. Solid core timber doors are usually capable of achieving this level of insulation. It is also good practice to include compressible seals in these doors in order to reduce sound transmission.

12.3 Building layout

THE FOLLOWING ADVICE OUTLINED in Figures 12.1 and 12.2 would hold true for any building design, but it is particularly relevant to the design of housing or rooms for residential purpose where the aim is to reduce the magnitude of noise being transmitted from one part of a building to another.

Table 12.2 Domestic sound insulation requirements around the world for new-build constructions (COST, 2013)

Country	Airborne performance parameter	Apartment/flat (dB)	Terraced house (dB)	Impact performance requirement	Apartment/flat (dB)	Terraced house (dB)
Austria	$D_{nT,w}$	>55	>60	$L'_{nT,w}$	<48	<46
Australia	$D_{nT,w}$ +Ctr	>45	>45	$L'_{nT,w}$ + CI	<62	–
Belgium	$D_{nT,w}$	>54	>58	$L'_{nT,w}$	<58	<50
Bulgaria	R'_w	>53	>53	L'_{nw}	<53	<53
Canada[1]	STC/ASTC	>50/47	>50/47	IIC	>50	–
Croatia	R'_w	>52	>52	L'_w	<68	<68
Czech Rep	R'_w	>53	>57	L'_{nw}	<55	<48
Denmark	R'_w	>55	>55	L'_{nw}	<53	<53
Ireland	$D_{nT,w}$	>53	>53	$L'_{nT,w}$	<61	–
England and Wales	$D_{nT,w}$ +Ctr	>45	>45	$L'_{nT,w}$ + CI	<62	–
Estonia	R'_w	>55	>55	L'_{nw}	<53	<53
Finland	R'_w	>55	>55	L'_{nw}	<53	<53
France	$D_{nT,w}$+C	>53	>53	$L'_{nT,w}$	<58	<58
Germany	R'_w	>53	>57	L_{nw}	<53	<48
Hungary	R'_w+C	>51	>56	L'_{nw}	<55	<45
Iceland	R'_w	>55	>55	L'_{nw}	<53	<53
Italy	R'_w	>50	>50	L'_{nw}	<63	<63
Latvia	R'_w	>54	>54	L'_{nw}	<54	<54
Lithuania	D_{nw} or R'_w	>55	>55	L'_{nw}	<53	<53
Netherlands	R'_w+C	>52	>52	$L'_{nT,w}$ + CI	<54	<54
New Zealand	STC	>55	>55	IIC	>55	–

Country						
Northern Ireland	$D'_{nT,w}$	>53	>53	$L'_{nT,w}$	<61	–
Norway	R'_w	>55	>55	L'_{nw}	<53	<53
Poland	R'_w+C	>50	>52	L'_{nw}	<58	<53
Portugal	$D_{n,w}$	>50	>50	L'_{nw}	<60	<60
Romania	R'_w	>51	>51	L'_{nw}	<59	<59
Russia	Ib	>50	–	Iy	<67	–
Scotland	$D_{nT,w}$	>56	>56	$L'_{nT,w}$	<56	–
Serbia	R'_w	>52	>52	L'_{nw} or $L'_{nT,w}$	<68	<68
Slovakia	R'_w or $D_{nT,w}$	>53	>57	L'_{nw} or $L'_{nT,w}$	<55	<48
Slovenia	R'_w	>52	>52	L'_{nw}	<58	<58
Spain	$DnT,A = D_{nT,w}+C$	>50	>50	$L'_{nT,w}$	<65	<65
Sweden	$R'_w+C50-3150$	>53	>53	$L'_{nw}+Ci,50-3150$	<56	<56
Switzerland	$D_{nT,w}+C$	>52	>55	$L'_{nT,w} + Ci$	<53	<50
United States*	STC	>50 (45)+	>50 (45)	IIC	>50(45)+	–

[1] As per proposed changes 2013

*United States guidelines for federal housing; state guidelines may differ

+ First value is for laboratory test data; value shown in brackets for on-site testing

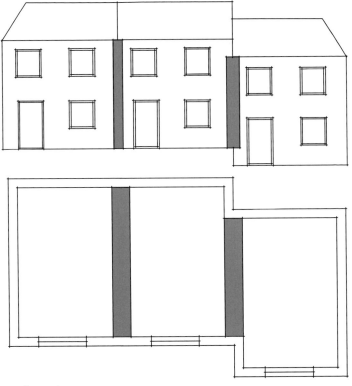

12.1 Steps and staggers

- Steps and staggers between noise-sensitive buildings can help improve sound insulation by reducing the effective area of common wall.
- Minimum steps and staggers of 1 ft (30 cm) should be considered if included for acoustic performance reasons.
- Steps and staggers of this size or greater can improve performance by up to 6 dB.
- Stack rooms so that noise-sensitive spaces are above one another. Avoid placing kitchens above or below bedrooms.
- Cluster around a central stair well so that areas of common walls are limited in size.

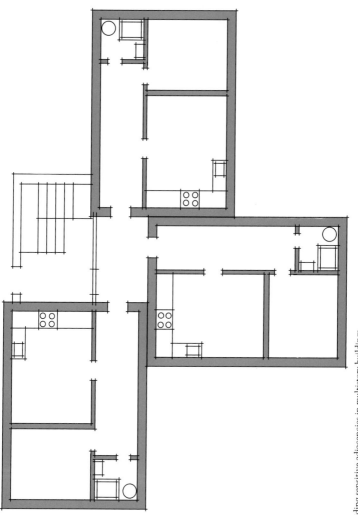

12.2 Avoiding sensitive adjacencies in multistory buildings

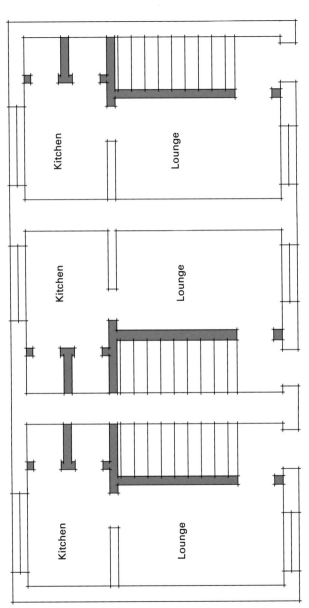

12.3 Handling of adjacent rooms

- Design layouts so that noisy activities back on to less sensitive areas (e.g., kitchens to circulation).
- Situate noise-sensitive spaces such as bedrooms as far from other dwellings as possible.
- Place stairwells and lift shafts as remote from noise-sensitive areas as possible.
- Noise from common circulation spaces can be further reduced by separating the stairwell from the entrance lobby to the dwellings on each floor with a glazed screen and door.

Advice specific to individual building types is given in other sections of Part II of the book, but for general layouts within dwellings Figure 12.3 offers some basic guidance.

- Use stairwells, circulation, and cupboard space as buffer zones between noise-sensitive rooms such as lounges and bedrooms. Limiting direct adjacencies of noise-sensitive spaces is preferred.
- Where adjacencies are unavoidable, place quiet rooms back-to-back and noisy rooms back-to-back (e.g., kitchen to kitchens, and lounges to lounges).

12.4 Specifying acoustic treatments

12.4.1 Identifying good materials or products for reducing sound transmission

When selecting suitable acoustic lining systems to use on a floor or wall, such as bonded resilient coverings, floating floor treatments (batten, cradle, or deck overlay systems), or resilient bar lining systems, manufacturers should prove that their systems can meet minimum standards based on laboratory data.

In this instance, the ΔL_w or ΔR_w parameters are used. This is the level of improvement a system has achieved when tested on a base timber or concrete floor under laboratory conditions. Regardless of whether it is an impact (ΔL_w) or airborne (ΔR_w) result the Δ character means that the higher the value, the better the performance. The minimum requirement for each lining system is listed below:

- Bonded resilient coverings on concrete floors – ΔL_w 17 dB
- Floating floor treatments on concrete floors – ΔR_w 5 dB; ΔL_w 22 dB
- Floating floor treatments on timber floors – ΔR_w 17 dB; $\Delta R_{w+}C_{tr}$ 13 dB; ΔL_w 16 dB
- Resilient ceiling bars on timber floors – ΔR_w 16 dB; $\Delta R_{w+}C_{tr}$ 14 dB; ΔL_w 16 dB.

12.4.2 Refurbishment and remedial treatments

Acoustically treating existing walls and floors is an incredibly complex task and would justify an entire book in itself. It is not uncommon to find that treatments that worked well on one development do not provide the same performance on other developments. This is primarily due to changes in existing detailing or variations in the integrity of the existing floor or wall. There are, however, some basic rules of thumb that can be applied:

- Independent linings to walls or ceiling (e.g., self-supporting metal stud, quilt, and a plasterboard lining) should provide better levels of acoustic insulation than a lining system which is fixed back to the existing wall or floor.
- The deeper the cavity depth created by a wall or ceiling lining, the better it will perform. Minimum depths of 4 in (100 mm) are suggested.

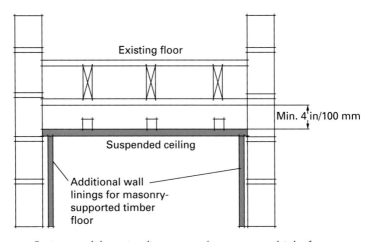

12.4 Section – remedial acoustic ceiling treatment of masonry-supported timber floors

- Placing mineral fiber within open cavities in a wall or floor should improve performance (suggested densities of 10–36 kg/m^3) and it is always recommended.
- Masonry-supported timber floors that are to be converted into separating floors between dwellings often suffer from flanking transmission problems, so it may be necessary to allow for the lining of load-bearing walls (e.g., metal lining frame, quilt, and plasterboard).
- Retaining original finishes can often be beneficial. Lath and plaster ceilings and existing ash deafening/pugging between joists on pre-1920s constructions provide significant acoustic benefit and should be retained where possible.

12.4.3 Avoiding risk when detailing partitions for dwellings

The following outlines good practice in the design of separating walls and floors between dwellings:

- Masonry wall constructions which incorporate twin leaf walls are preferable to single leaf constructions. Minimum cavity depths of 4 in (100 mm) between leaves are best, as is the use of very lightweight wall ties. Block work with higher densities tend to perform best.
- Only where single leaf constructions include a metal or timber stud lining system with fiber insulation and plasterboard finishes can similar insulation levels be achievable.
- Twin independent timber or metal stud systems can be suitable for walls between dwellings, assuming each leaf is independent. Internal cavity depths of 9½ in (240 mm) are preferable. Double layers of plasterboard and fiber insulation within the cavity are required.
- The use of fiber insulation within any wall cavity should include instructions for the material to be stapled or held in place, to avoid sagging during the lifetime of the wall.
- Cast in-situ concrete floors tend to require less detailing in order to avoid sound leakage paths. Where pre-cast slabs are used, the inclusion of a poured concrete topping or screed will ensure better performance levels.
- Concrete floor slabs are inherently good at controlling airborne sound but will require either an isolated floor treatment and/or a suspended or isolated ceiling treatment to control impact sound.

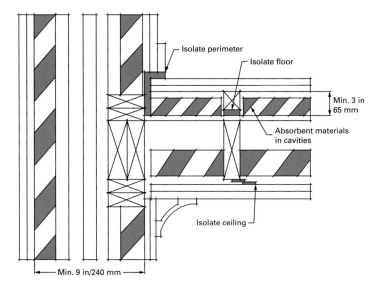

12.5 Section through floor/wall junction – good detailing practice for timber kit separating floors

■ Timber floor structures can provide good levels of insulation but are reliant on isolation layers being applied to both the top and bottom of the structural floor (e.g., floating floors and isolated or suspended ceiling systems).

■ Anything which bridges a cavity within a separating floor or wall can result in increased sound transmission. This includes mortar buildup within wall cavities, service runs through floors, failure to isolate floating floors at the perimeter, and continuous load-bearing elements such as walls and columns.

■ Avoid locating elevator/lift shafts on walls that are common to living rooms or bedrooms.

Further reading

Building Research Establishment (BRE) and Construction Industry Research and Information Association (CIRIA) (1993) *Sound control for homes*. Englewood, CO: IHS/BRE Press.

BREEAM (2009) *BREEAM 2010 Code for sustainable homes – technical guide. Version 2.* BRE Global: Watford.

COST (2013) *Towards a common framework … in building acoustics throughout Europe.* COST Action TU0901 final conference, Copenhagen, December 2013.

Robust Details (2013) *Robust Details* handbook. Milton Keynes: Robust Details Ltd.

Smith, S. et al. (2006) *Housing and sound insulation, improving existing attached dwellings and designing for conversions.* London: Arcamedia.

chapter 13

Commercial

13.1 The importance of good acoustics in commercial buildings

THE CONSIDERATION OF ACOUSTIC DESIGN in commercial buildings is often overlooked; yet, in commercial environments such as cinemas, it is one of the key design features. This is because the people who operate cinemas know that being able to hear the film is almost as important as being able to see it. In essence they have a product which they hope to show off in as favorable manner as possible. The publication *Sound Business* by Julian Treasure, and the creation of the international organization the Audio Branding Academy, are clear indicators that businesses are beginning to use sound as a means to enhance their sales as well as the perception of their products. This can have direct links to the built environment and it should be the aim of any designer to either provide a space that is as acoustically neutral as possible to allow a business to add their own identity, or tailor a space for the specific needs of a business and its customers.

Behind this new area of acoustic design there are also the key requirements of providing suitable working environments for staff, avoiding disturbance to neighboring properties, and meeting the expectations of the end user. As this can be a particularly complex subject area, this chapter will set out some of the more basic design rules and cover a selection of the most common commercial environments.

13.2 Performance criteria

13.2.1 Defining the acoustic environment

The level of acoustic performance for a commercial space will be dependent upon four key design factors:

1) The expected use of the space – what activities will take place there and the underlying requirements to achieve this expectation.

2) The comfort and wellbeing of staff – the most obvious being control of excessive noise levels to avoid hearing loss, but there can also be correlations between staff productivity and inappropriate noise environments.

3) The noise impact on existing neighbors – noise created by commercial activities is not uncommon and can be a significant part of any design work required to show compliance with national and local requirements that protect existing amenity.

4) The expectations of the end user – this can often differ considerably from the basic expected requirement; for example, a room may be designed as a space in which to eat, but the end user may also expect it to be a suitable place to talk or listen to live music.

The first three design factors are normally set as part of any design brief to ensure that minimum statutory requirements are achieved or a basic level of comfort is provided.

The final key design factor is often achieved as a result of luck or chance, but it is probably reasonable to assume that in most situations the aim is to create an environment in which there is a sense of privacy without isolation. For example, people tend to feel comfortable in cafés/restaurants where they can easily hear and understand the people they are talking to but do not want to be overheard or understood by other groups in the room. Similarly, people tend to prefer retail environments where there is a sufficiently diffuse and constant background noise level so that they do not feel they are under scrutiny by other shoppers or shop assistants, but not so noisy that they are distracted or discouraged from extended browsing. Of course, there are obvious exceptions to these rules but these tend to be integral to the type of client that a business is trying to attract. Some retailers purposefully create a sound environment akin to a loud bar or disco to attract young shoppers and exclude older shoppers, while some bars set playlist policies for music and style to define themselves a place for people with a particular taste.

13.2.2 Specification targets

Appendix B details minimum ambient noise, mechanical noise, and reverberation time requirements for a range of commercial spaces. There is limited guidance on the control of sound transmission in commercial spaces, with the exception of cinema design; however, Chapter 14 outlines the requirements for hotels and can provide a good starting point for other commercial developments (e.g., bars/clubs). Any consideration of the control of sound insulation should also look to the guidance given in Section 6.4 regarding perceived levels of sound insulation.

The following provides an outline for where sound insulation should be considered:

- Any room which is created as a treatment space (such as within a day spa) should provide a good level of speech privacy between it and any other room (around STC/R$_w$ 45–50 dB). Where the treatment is medical in nature (e.g., dentists, optometrists), these levels should be increased to insulation levels comparable with those detailed for healthcare environments (see Chapter 8).
- Locating rooms with lots of bass-intensive noise (e.g., amplified music) close to rooms which are for more intimate activities (e.g., dining) will require high levels of sound insulation (around STC/R$_w$ 55–60 dB). Note that total control of noise is not guaranteed.
- High-end retail environments or places where customers will be discussing significant sums of money or personal details (jewelry shops, car showrooms, banks) should allow for withdrawn rooms which provide high levels of confidentiality (STC/R$_w$ 50 dB min).
- Partitions separating general retail space or retail units (e.g., open-fronted shops within a mall or within a department store) should provide minimum insulation values of STC/R$_w$ 45 dB. Levels of STC/R$_w$ 50–55 dB should be seen as a minimum for entirely separate retail units which open out into the street (e.g., strip mall).

Note: These insulation requirements can be reduced in environments where background noise levels are kept artificially high (e.g., music or noise masking), although the use of such noise may not always be appropriate for the commercial setting.

13.3 Design guidelines

THE FOLLOWING SECTION HAS BEEN SET OUT with topic headings based on particular commercial/retail environments. As this is a wide topic area, each building type cannot be discussed in detail, so only key points have been included.

13.3.1 Outdoor eating/drinking areas

The primary concern with outdoor space is the impact of noise from these spaces on surrounding noise-sensitive locations, with a secondary concern regarding the comfort of the users.

In order to minimize noise impact from outdoor eating and drinking areas, where they are overlooked by noise-sensitive locations (e.g., dwellings), as well as improve user comfort, the following advice is offered:

■ Avoid placing such areas within 65 ft (20 m) of any dwelling.

■ Where such areas are affiliated to noisy commercial activities (such as bars or nightclubs with high levels of amplified music), ensure that there is significant separation between noisy internal areas and the external space. Access via long corridors or multiple doors between such areas is recommended.

■ Provide seating layouts of two to four people per table. Avoid large group seating arrangements, particularly for spaces used at nighttime. Smaller groupings usually mean people will interact more quietly.

■ Orient seating layouts so that as many users as possible face away from any noise-sensitive location.

■ High-backed seating or seating with overhead canopies can be used to create intimate pockets and reduce overall noise levels.

■ Avoiding the provision of seats in outdoor smoking areas has been seen as a means to limit noise, however it can have the opposite effect of encouraging people to congregate in larger groups. Providing limited seating for outdoor smoking areas can limit the formation of larger groups.

■ Where possible, provide screening between an outdoor seating area and a noise-sensitive location. Ideally an acoustic barrier (e.g., a fence or wall) with minimum height of 6 ft (1.8 m) in close proximity to the outdoor seating area can be effective, but even visual screening can help to limit the perception of noise on nearby residents.

- Where weather conditions allow, soft cushioning to seating should be encouraged.
- Locating external seating areas in enclosed courtyards can result in significant disturbance where noise-sensitive locations overlook a courtyard, and should be avoided.
- The introduction of vegetation (grass, shrubs, wall-climbing plants) can go some way to provide acoustic absorption within courtyard space, but performance will be limited.
- Amplified music in such areas should be avoided. If it is to be used, it should be seen as a background source. The use of small loudspeakers set in multiple locations is preferable to fewer, larger loudspeakers.
- Management of such spaces is key, and careful consideration should be given to the need for external eating or drinking areas which are to be used after 9:00PM.

13.3.2 Bars and nightclubs

There are three key areas for consideration when dealing with acoustics in bars and nightclubs:

a) protecting the hearing of the employees
b) ensuring the control of noise break-out to noise-sensitive locations around the bar or club
c) creating a good environment for the users.

Noise levels in some bars and nightclubs can exceed guidance levels issued for the protection of hearing (see Table 3.1). In some instances the approach taken by governments is that when people choose to enter such environments they do so at their own risk, but for employees the element of choice is removed and so it is incumbent upon the owners to ensure protection. This can often only be achieved through limiting shift patterns for key workers; however, there are some good guidance methods that should be adopted as part of general design. Figure 13.1 shows a proposed layout for a bar with provision for live or amplified music.

1) Grid represents location of loudspeaker system over small dance floor for use with DJ. It is now possible to specify flat-panel speakers and/or directional speaker systems to reduce noise build up across the space.

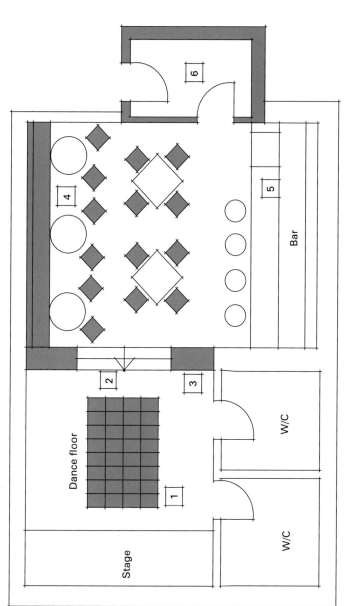

13.1 Possible bar/club layout for controlling high noise levels (adapted from HSE, 2008)

2) Change in floor level helps to reduce effective open areas between high-noise space (stage/dance floor) and seating areas.

3) Area for live or amplified music is separated from the main bar area by shielding with fin walls and/or bulkhead details. This can limit buildup of noise in areas where staff spend the majority of their time.

4) High-backed banked or booth seating is upholstered to provide absorption. This can be taken up to ceiling height. Remaining seating is also upholstered, to provide further absorption within the main bar area.

5) Bar is located as far as possible from high-noise area around stage/dance floor. There is no direct line of sight between bar and high-noise area. Mobile staff such as glass collectors, servers, or security staff can then be put on rotating shifts so their exposure to high-noise areas is limited.

6) Double door entrance lobby provided, to control noise break-out (see Figure 13.2 for further details).

Controlling noise break-out from bars and nightclubs can be a significant issue and it is not uncommon for the operational licences for a bar or club to be revoked if the level of complaints with regards to noise is sufficiently high. The following sets out some guidance on controlling noise break-out, assuming noise-sensitive locations are within close proximity (i.e., dwellings within 330 ft/100 m):

■ Nightclubs should not be located within buildings that are structurally connected to any noise-sensitive location (e.g., dwellings).

■ Bars can be located within buildings that are structurally connected to noise-sensitive locations (e.g., dwellings) if there is no desire to provide live music or karaoke. Where dwellings are directly above, careful consideration should be given to whether the location is suitable depending on the anticipated style of bar. Even in a bar with no music there should still be an acceptance that separating partitions will have to be upgraded.

■ When controlling noise from a bar to an adjoining dwelling, it is likely that acoustic treatments of separating floors, separating walls, external walls, and load-bearing elements (columns, beams, flanking walls) will be required.

■ As a general rule of thumb, designers should expect the need to independently line all structural elements such as wall, floors, columns, and beams. This normally takes the form of metal or timber framing systems with multiple plasterboard linings. It is preferable that the core structural elements are specified as heavy mass constructions (concrete floors, high-density block walls).

- Noise break-out via glazing can be a significant issue. It is preferable for nightclubs to avoid the inclusion of windows in favor of mechanical ventilation systems that include acoustic attenuation to the ducted system.

- For bars which are to have significant live or amplified music, glazing designs should allow for significantly heavy double glazing systems (e.g., twin layers of laminated glass) along with additional secondary glazing systems.

- Glazing designs should allow for cavity depths between double glazing and secondary glazing units of at least 8 in/200mm. Such systems should be fixed glazing with compressible rubberized seals, with an allowance for the windows to be operable for cleaning purposes.

- Acoustically absorptive reveals between double and secondary glazing units should be considered. This can be achieved by lining the reveals with mineral fiber ceiling tiles.

- Ventilation systems are likely to be required, and provision should be made for significant attenuation works. This is likely to require acoustically lined ducts of 3–6 ft (1–2 m) in length, along with cowls to direct ventilation outlets and inlets away from noise-sensitive locations.

- Acoustic lobbies to entrances and exits should be incorporated in order to reduce noise break-out, as detailed in Figure 13.2.

- External walls to the lobby should be either a twin leaf, high-density masonry construction or masonry with an independent inner stud system lined with multiple high-density plasterboard linings.

- It is preferable to design the lobby so that it is within the main curtilage of the building. Concrete roof constructions provide the best performance where an entrance lobby extends from the main curtilage of the building. Pitched roof systems with mineral fiber materials packed within the cavities and multiple high-density plasterboard linings can also be effective. Comments on roof structures are given in Chapter 4.

- Doors should be oriented so that, even when both are open, there is no clear line of sight from inside to outside.

- Doors should be fitted with self-closing mechanisms.

- Ideally the lobby should be sufficiently deep so that one door can fully close before the second door is opened.

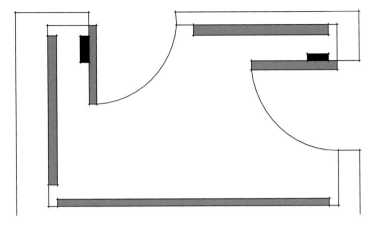

13.2 Acoustic entrance lobby

- Doors should be either solid core timber or metal lined doors. Minimum performance levels of STC/R_w 35 dB should be considered for both doors, including any glazing set within the door.
- The lobby should be lined with acoustically absorptive materials in order to reduce noise buildup. Wall-mounted fabric panels, acoustically absorptive ceiling tiles, and heavy wearing carpets should be considered.

Providing a good acoustic environment should be based on customer preference, but it can often be dictated by staff preferences or organizational preferences. It is assumed that in nightclubs customers prefer to be in an environment with loud bass-intensive music, while in local bars the preference may be for a quiet environment in which to chat. However, preferences may vary from customer to customer or from one night to another. The following should be considered in the design of bars and nightclubs.

- The provision of quieter areas should be allowed for in any bar or nightclub, particularly where there is a desire to appeal to as wide a demographic as possible.
- Avoiding the placement of loudspeakers near the bar area so that customers can easily give drinks/food orders, thereby improving customer service and efficiency.

■ Louder or quieter areas can be achieved by zoning amplified music systems, or through separating activities as shown in Figure 13.1.

■ Entrance lobbies to nightclubs are an effective way of controlling noise break-out, but they can also help building a sense of anticipation for customers as music levels increase when they approach the main club area.

■ Sound quality from amplified music within a club or bar will be improved where rooms have an even distribution of diffuse surfaces. Paneling, ornamentation, and furniture can all add to room diffusion.

■ Where there is a design preference for smooth surface finishes, consideration should be given to creating rooms of non-standard shapes, i.e., avoid simple square or rectangular rooms.

■ Where there is a preference for simple square or rectangular rooms, consideration should be given to well-distributed absorptive finishes, e.g., wall panels, ceiling-mounted absorption, or carpets.

13.3.3 Restaurants, cafés, and kitchens

Noise break-out issues associated with cafés and restaurants are generally associated with noise from kitchens, mechanical ventilation, and air extract. Noise levels within areas used for customers to eat are usually sufficiently low to not cause a problem when protecting staff hearing. The issue of customer comfort is associated with the provision of an environment which has sufficient high background noise levels to give a sense of privacy for each group of diners and the avoidance of high-noise events that may cause distraction.

When considering noise break-out from kitchens, the following good practice is recommended:

■ Impact sounds (chopping, footfall, etc.) are a particular issue. Locating kitchens above noise-sensitive locations should be avoided, i.e., do not place commercial kitchens above dwellings, hotel bedrooms, treatment rooms, offices, or meeting rooms.

■ Design of good noise control to ventilation and air extract systems is imperative. The NR/NC requirements stated in Appendix B provide a guide on adequate control levels, both within kitchens and for surrounding rooms and building types.

■ There should be an allowance in any mechanical system design for the inclusion of acoustic treatments such as attenuated duct work, resilient mounts, and acoustic louvers. This is a specialist design area, so it should be subcontracted to an appropriate contractor.

■ In order to maintain suitable NR/NC requirements within a commercial kitchen, ventilation systems should have a maximum supply air velocity of 10 ft/s (3 m/s) and a maximum return velocity of 13 ft/s (4 m/s).

■ Locate fridge/freezer units, ovens, burners, and benchtop electrical equipment away from any adjoining wall between a kitchen and a noise-sensitive location (e.g., dwellings, hotel bedrooms).

■ The location of external waste and recycling areas should be as far from any noise-sensitive location as possible. It is generally good practice to screen these areas, so there is no direct line of sight to any noise-sensitive location.

■ It is good practice to separate kitchens from dining areas with partitions that provide a minimum insulation value of STC/R_w 50 dB.

■ In instances where there is a desire to be able to view the kitchen from the dining area, limit the open area of any viewing aperture, avoid floor-to-ceiling openings, consider partial or complete screening of any opening with double glazed units, and locate noisy equipment (ovens, burners, benchtop electrical equipment) as far from the viewing aperture as possible.

■ Providing corridors to separate direct access from a kitchen to a dining area should be considered to reduce noise break-out during serving.

When considering noise control within restaurant or café dining areas, the following guidelines are suggested:

■ Diners in restaurants and cafés tend to assume an environment that will be suitable for speech communication without interruption from other diners or other noise sources. Guidelines on suitable ambient noise levels and reverberation times are given in Appendix B.

■ Where there is a preference for hard floor finishes (timber, laminate, concrete, tile), it should be accepted that noise levels will quickly build up. This can be offset with the use of upholstered seating and soft furnishings, wall-mounted absorptive panels, and even tablecloths.

■ Areas of hard flooring around bars, serving stations and self-service cutlery/condiment stations should have rubber matting placed over the floor in order to reduce noise from any dropped glasses, dishes, or cutlery.

- The use of background music should be considered to provide masking from the conversation from other diners where background noise levels are low (i.e., below L_{Aeq} 35 dB) and where room reverberation times are at or below 0.8 seconds.

- Background music in areas where reverberation times are higher can be appropriate dependent on the style of restaurant being created (e.g., rock-oriented cafés where people expect louder music).

- Where noise control levels of NC/NR 35 or below are set within a room, systems should have a maximum supply air velocity of 5 ft/s (1.5 m/s) and a maximum return velocity of 6.5 ft/s (2m/s). This would be akin to ventilation to a restaurant area.

- Where noise control levels of NC/NR 40 or below are set within a room, systems should have a maximum supply air velocity of 8 ft/s (2.5 m/s) and a maximum return velocity of 10 ft/s (3m/s). This would be akin to ventilation to a café.

- Placing cowls or absorptive wall and ceiling linings around coffee/espresso machines can help reduce steam jet and banging noise. However, it should be recognized that this noise is associated with cafés and fresh coffee, so it is not always preferable to completely eliminate this noise. For restaurants or fine dining, these machines should be located well away from the diners. For cafés they should be visible and include the recommended treatments.

1.3.5 Cinema

Cinema design is a highly specialized area of acoustics and it is always considered best practice to engage the services of an acoustician on such projects. The following sets out current design guidelines on achieving shell stage design.

- In order to control external noise, it is recommended that cinemas are not constructed in locations where maximum external noise levels regularly exceed $L_{Amax(s)}$ 80 dB.

- Minimum façade insulation levels of STC/R_w 45 dB should be achieved. See Figure 13.4 for details on possible specifications.

- Guidelines on permissible ambient noise levels, mechanical noise levels, and reverberation times are given in Appendix B, along with guidelines on suitable door specifications.

- External walls, roof constructions, and structural elements must not be continuous from one auditorium to another.
- External walls and roof constructions are likely to require lining with an acoustically shielded construction, as shown in Figure 13.3.
- Floor slabs to projection rooms should ideally be concrete slab constructions with a minimum weight of 300 kg/m^2 and a maximum permitted dead load deflection of ¼ in (5 mm).
- For new developments, partitions which separate cinema auditoriums from adjoining commercial activities are likely to require additional acoustic treatments (e.g., suspended ceiling treatments where bars are located below auditorium), particularly where amplified music is expected within the adjoining commercial space.
- For new developments, it is also anticipated that any mechanical room or noisy equipment associated with an adjoining commercial activity will need to be located well away from any auditorium.
- Service penetrations which pass through auditorium walls should be avoided completely.
- Where service penetrations through auditorium floors are unavoidable, they should be independently lined with triple layers of high-density plasterboard and lagged with mineral fiber insulation along their entire length.
- Raked seating and floor finishes to auditoriums should be isolated from the structural floor and separating walls. The preference is for concrete slab or screed constructions set on resilient isolation layers.
- Ensure that escalators and lifts/elevators do not share a common wall with the cinema auditorium.

Table 13.1 outlines minimum insulation levels for good shell stage cinema design.

Figure 13.3 is a suitable separating wall detail showing appropriate detailing for the wall head and wall foot.

- Include a break in the roof liner tray.
- Allow for a deflection head detail at wall head sealed with a flexible gypsum-based caulk.
- Suspended ceiling details are required and should include mineral fiber quilt with minimum three layers of high-density plasterboard. Where boards meet wall, seal any gap with a flexible gypsum-based caulk.

Table 13.1 Cinema partitions, performance guidelines (pre-owner's fit-out/shell stage)

Partition	Minimum STC/R_w	Comment
Auditorium to auditorium	72	Any wall/floor used should also be able to achieve a minimum reduction of 45 dB at 63 Hz
Auditorium to concession	62	Concession includes any food serving, bar, or corridor around an auditorium
Auditorium to projection room	60	It is assumed that, due to the need for an aperture in the projection room wall, this could not be tested on site
Projection room to concession	57	Concession includes any food serving, bar, or corridor around an auditorium
Auditorium to store/escape stairs	52	Including under-croft below raked seating
Auditorium to staff areas/bathrooms	57	It is preferable to locate toilets away from auditorium areas
Auditorium to adjoining commercial activities (restaurant/bar)	72	Any wall/floor used should also be able to achieve a minimum reduction of 45 dB at 63 Hz

- Stud work and plasterboard to be set on a resilient layer. This can be a bituminous-based felt or a closed cell foam material.
- Floating concrete screed details are advised. Screed is laid over a high-performance resilient mount capable of providing acoustic isolation under high loads.
- Screed and permanent shuttering isolated from separating wall with an isolation strip.
- Separating wall lined either side with minimum four layers high-density board, preferably of varying thicknesses, and twin layers of mineral fiber quilt within the cavity. Mineral fiber may require stapling into position to avoid sagging in the cavity, or to be fitted on a supporting net or chicken wire.

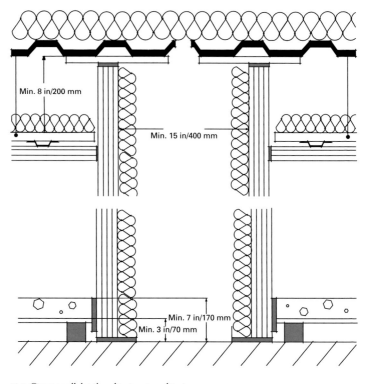

13.3 Cinema wall detail, auditorium to auditorium

Figure 13.4 shows a suitable detail for controlling flanking noise at the external façade. Here it is assumed that the external leaf of the external wall is masonry but a cladding system would also be acceptable.

■ Locate expansion joint to inner external leaf of masonry behind separating wall detail to break the continuous line of the block work. The gap should be filled with a flexible water-resistant seal.

■ Where the plasterboard to the wall that separates the auditorium meets the external wall, any gaps should be made good with a flexible gypsum-based caulk.

■ The inner leaf of the external wall should be lined with an independent

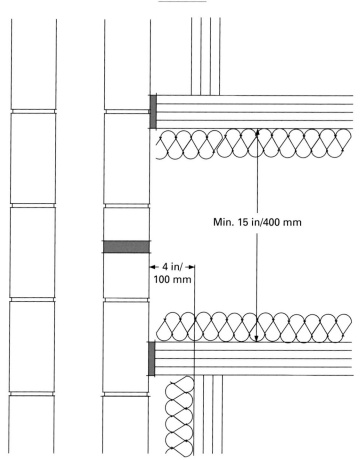

13.4 External wall detail for cinemas, auditorium to outside

stud frame, set a minimum of 5/12 in (10 mm) from the block work wall. A minimum cavity depth of 4 in (100 mm) should be provided.

■ The plasterboard lining to the external wall should be minimum three layers of high-density plasterboard.

■ A layer of high-density mineral fiber quilt should be placed within the cavity created by the external wall lining. Mineral fiber may require stapling into position to avoid sagging in the cavity, or be fitted on a supporting net or chicken wire.

Further reading

DEFRA (2005) *Guidance on the control of odour and noise from commercial kitchen exhaust systems*. London: DEFRA/HMSO.

HSE (2005) *Controlling noise at work, the control of noise at work regulations 2005*. London: Health and Safety Executive/HSE Books.

HSE (2008) *Sound advice. Control of noise at work in music and entertainment*. London: Health and Safety Executive/HSE Books.

Lothian, S. (2008) *Smoking outdoors and noise survey*. Edinburgh: Edinburgh Napier University.

RICS (2012) *SKA rating scheme*. London: RICS.

chapter 14

Hotels

14.1 The importance of good acoustics in hotels

WITH MANY HOTELS OFFERING GUARANTEES of a good night's sleep, the control of sound is of paramount importance even in budget hotels. However, each of the major hotel chains takes a different approach to how they specify acoustic performance, so there are real dangers for the design team. For example, one hotel chain may require airborne sound insulation to be assessed against STCs, while another may assess against $D_{nT,w} + C_{tr}$.

As well as a variety of on-site performance parameters, each hotel chain sets differing performance criteria and it is not sufficient to assume that a higher-rated hotel will automatically require higher levels of sound insulation between rooms. The good night guarantee for budget hotels can mean that they set higher standards than more prestigious hotel chains.

This chapter provides examples of good practice across the hotel industry. The performance standards that are included have been gleaned from a variety of hotel design projects, taking the most onerous standards to define best practices and outline key areas to watch out for when involved in the design of any hotel.

14.2 Performance standards

14.2.1 Performance specifications

Acoustic performance levels in hotels are dictated by a number of key factors. With regards to sound insulation between rooms, the most strict criteria would be required:

■ if a hotel is likely to be used regularly by guests who need to sleep during the day, e.g., hotels near an airport which are to be used by flight crews

■ if the hotel chain wishes to offer a money-back guarantee for guests who do not get an uninterrupted night's sleep.

The most strict controls on ambient noise levels are more likely to be required:

■ if a hotel is to be located within a noisy city center location close to high transportation noise
■ if a hotel is to include large function suites or hopes to gain a significant portion of its income from bars and restaurants open to non-residential guests.

Specific guidance levels for ambient noise control, acceptable mechanical noise levels, maximum permissible reverberation times, and airborne and impact insulation requirements are detailed in Appendix B.

14.2.2 Maximum permissible noise levels from external sources

It is often expected that maximum permissible noise levels are applied in hotel design to avoid disturbance from infrequent high-noise events such as may be common in an urban location (delivery noise, people shouting in the street). Suitable levels are detailed in Table 14.1. Particular care should be taken when applying a maximum noise criterion and discussions with the client should be sought at the design stage. This is because it can often be impractical or extremely costly to achieve the control of sudden or very loud noise events.

The following guidance should be applied when considering the use of control standards on maximum noise levels or L_{Amax}:

■ Function rooms – L_{Amax} for function rooms are generally only applicable if there is an expectation that the function room is to be used for lectures, conferences, or other events where public speaking is anticipated.
■ Guest bedrooms – The L_{Amax} criteria for guest bedrooms is commonly only applied during the nighttime period.
■ Frequency of high-noise events – when assessing L_{Amax} it is anticipated that it should apply to regular occurrences (e.g., events that would occur more than 10 times during the night (11:00PM–7:00AM). Therefore unless the hotel is next to a fire or police station, then sirens from emergency service vehicles should be discounted.

■ High-noise environments – In very high noise environments, such as city center locations or next to airports, the application of the L_{Amax} criterion can become impractical to achieve, particularly when dealing with the conversions of existing buildings. In such instances, the L_{Amax} criterion should be relaxed; a –10 dB reduction in the standard performance level is a good rule of thumb.

■ Naturally ventilated buildings – The use of naturally ventilated designs is popular due to their eco-friendly benefits; however, the use of natural ventilation is at odds with the control of noise break-in to a hotel. If existing noise levels on a hotel development site exceed an L_{Aeq} (night-time) of 62 dB and/or an L_{Amax} of 72 dB, then it can be assumed that mechanical ventilation will be required.

14.2.3 Noise limits for heavy rain

Noise from heavy rainfall can also be a cause of disturbance within hotel developments. It is likely that such an issue would only be of concern for rooms on the top floor of a hotel or where the hotel is only a single story in height. Here the application of the NR or NC parameter is suitable, and the required performance levels are detailed in Table 14.1.

Table 14.1 Control levels for various noise sources – hotel

Room	External sources (Section 14.2.2)	Rain noise (Section 14.2.3)	Lift/elevator noise (Section 14.2.4)
	$L_{Amax(f)}$ dB	NR/NC	$L_{Amax(f)}$ dB
Guest bedroom	40	40	25
Meeting room	45	45	30
Function room	50	45	30
Lounge	50	45	30
Bar	50	50	n/a
Restaurant	50	50	n/a
Lobby/foyer	55	50	50
Reception	55	50	50
Office	50	45	40

Table 14.2 Sound insulation performance requirements, hotel guest bedroom to hotel guest bedroom, depending on separating construction type

Construction type	Minimum R_w/STC (dB)
Reasonable performance levels	58
Good performance levels	63

14.2.4 Control of noise from lifts/elevators

Lift/elevator noise can be of concern particularly where there are limited opportunities to separate lifts/elevator and lifts/elevator lobbies from guest bedrooms. Suitable performance levels for hotels are detailed in Table 14.1.

14.2.5 Sound insulation between guest bedrooms within a hotel

The primary area of concern in any hotel is the partitions that separate one guest bedroom from another. Performance standards for airborne sound control, given in Table 14.2, depend on performance.

Performance levels for impact sound are detailed in Table B.1.

Note: Achieving "good" insulation levels is not in itself an absolute guarantee that guests will not be disturbed by noise. It is a performance level that ensures that most people would not be disturbed by noise from a neighboring room and reduces the risk to the hotel operator.

14.3 Design guidelines

14.3.1 Controlling external noise

The following guidance should be considered when appraising the orientation and layout of a hotel to control external noise break-in:

■ Orient guest bedrooms away from a direct line of sight to a significant noise source, e.g., road, industrial site.

■ Consider the use of fixed glazing and mechanical ventilation where external noise levels exceed L_{Aeq} 62 dB and/or $L_{Amax(f)}$ 72 dB at 3 ft (1 m) from the hotel façade.

■ Consider the use of primary and secondary glazing along with mechanical ventilation where external noise levels exceed L_{Aeq} 75 and/or $L_{Amax(f)}$

82 dB at 3 ft (1 m) from the hotel façade, e.g., for hotels located next to nightclubs, airports, or very busy roads.

- Do not locate guest bedrooms with a clear line of sight to a mechanical room or an area of rooftop units associated with the hotel itself.

- Do not place external smoking areas or external drinking and dining areas within 65 ft (20 m) of a guest bedroom window unless their use is restricted to between 10:00AM and 8:00pPM.

- Where hotels physically adjoin a residential dwelling, then minimum insulation levels in line with local building codes or standards should be applied.

- Where hotels physically adjoin a cinema, the minimum performance criterion should be an STC or R_w of 80 dB. Bedroom to cinema auditoria should always be avoided.

- Where hotels physically adjoin a retail space or bar, the minimum performance criterion should be an STC or R_w 70 dB. Locating guest bedrooms directly next to a bar or nightclub with bass-intensive music should always be avoided.

14.3.2 Control of internal noise

Guest bedrooms above hotel bars should be avoided where the hotel bar is open to the general public or is regularly used as a function bar. The location of guest bedrooms above restaurants, kitchens, mechanical rooms, and laundries may be permissible if insulation levels above STC/R_w 75 dB can be achieved.

Locating any of the following rooms above a guest bedroom should be avoided:

- bar
- restaurant
- lounge
- function hall
- fitness center
- public toilet/restroom
- spa
- kitchen
- stair
- laundry
- shop.

Note: If such adjacencies cannot be avoided, then a minimum requirement of FIIC 75 or $L'_{nT,w}$ 35 dB should be set. Achieving such levels of insulation is only likely to be possible with heavy concrete floor constructions which incorporate an acoustically isolated deep screed (196–328 ft or 60–100 m) finished with an impact reduction layer (matt and/or carpet) and an acoustically isolated ceiling. A typical minimum construction depth of 27 in (700 mm) would not be unusual.

Locating any of the following rooms next to (commonly separating wall) each other should be avoided:

- guest bedroom to function room
- guest bedroom to bar
- guest bedroom to kitchen
- guest bedroom to laundry
- guest bedroom to mechanical room
- guest bedroom to restaurant
- meeting room to kitchen
- meeting room to laundry
- meeting room to mechanical room.

The location of any of the following rooms next to a hotel meeting room will require appropriate room management by the hotel so that activities do not clash:

- bar
- function room
- spa
- fitness room
- guest bedroom
- restaurant.

- Do not place function rooms, bars, restaurants, kitchens, mechanical rooms, and laundries along the same common corridor with guest bedrooms.
- Do not place rooms with high-activity usage at the far end of a corridor which also has guest bedrooms along it, e.g., meeting rooms, spas, fitness rooms, laundries, etc.

- Place doors within corridors to screen off guest bedrooms from foyers or lift lobbies.
- Do not place fire doors along corridors within close proximity to the door of a guest bedroom. See Figure 14.1.If this cannot be avoided, then doors should be held open with magnetic doorstops, which can be deactivated in the event of a fire alarm.
- Fit corridor fire doors with soft-closing devices and fit brush seals to the doorframe.
- Do not provide areas in corridors outside guest bedrooms which entice guests to loiter or gather in groups, e.g., shoe shine, ice machines, seating. Such areas should always be separated from guest-room corridor runs by closed fire doors or located in lift/elevator lobbies.

Laying out bedrooms so that beds back onto beds and desk or wardrobe space backs onto desk/wardrobe space in the adjacent room can help reduce noise disturbance. Place air conditioning outlets as far from the bed head as possible.

Figure 14.2 details an optimum bedroom layout to reduce noise disturbance within a guest bedroom.

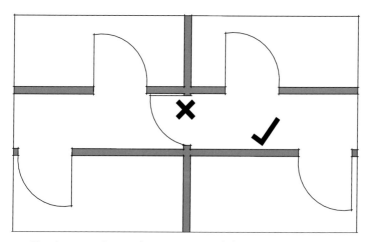

14.1 Place doors in corridors away from entrance to guest bedrooms

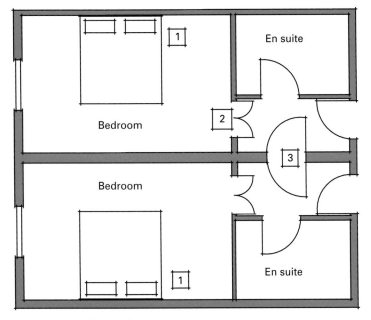

14.2 Optimum hotel bedroom layout

1)   Locate bedheads as far from entrance as possible.
2)   Door between bedroom area and en suite helps to reduce noise disturbance from corridor.
3)   Position access doors between rooms away from bedhead, creating an area that can be closed off, will help to reduce disturbance when adjoining rooms are not hired out under the same occupancy.

Interconnecting doors between bedrooms will always reduce the overall acoustic performance of the partition. Avoiding noise disturbance therefore becomes a key function of the management of adjoining rooms. For best results when the adjoining doors are not in use, the following is suggested:

■   A set of twin doors either side of the partition is always preferable.
■   The doors should be a solid core construction and be capable of achieving a minimum R_w/STC of 35 dB.

- Full perimeter seals, including drop seals at the bottom of each door, should be considered.
- Locate the adjoining doors as far as possible from the bedhead.

Hotel function rooms have to accommodate a variety of activities from conferences to amplified music events.

- If the hotel function room is likely to be located close to existing dwellings (i.e., within 130 ft/40 m), then it is likely that primary and secondary glazing will be required in function rooms expected to be used for live or amplified music. A standard double-glazed unit with a 4 in (100 mm) cavity and a secondary unit with a laminate glass (e.g., 1/3 in/8.8 mm) is common.
- Any bar associated with a function room should be located away from the intended location of any live or amplified music, to reduce risk to staff hearing.
- Where movable walls are used between function and meeting rooms, performance standards of above STC/R_w 55 dB should be sought from the manufacturer. Hotel operators should be made aware of the expected reduction in acoustic performance between fixed walls and movable walls. The need for flexibility of space should be weighed against the need for acoustic performance.

14.3.3 Avoiding risk – partition details

- Boxing around the rear of electrical sockets within separating walls with plasterboard or fitting putty pads to the rear of a socket box can reduce impact noise transmission through guest bedroom walls.
- Installing timber or plywood panels between metal or timber stud to offer additional structural support for headboards can reduce overall cavity depths of a guest-room wall. Allowances should be made for any reduction in cavity depth.
- Where timber or plywood panels are placed as an alternative to an inner layer of plasterboard, it is important that the board selected has the same surface density as the plasterboard being replaced.
- Electrical and mechanical services should be run along main corridors and fed into rooms via the corridor wall. Penetrations through partitions separating any noise-sensitive rooms should be avoided.

14.4 Specifications for controlling reverberation times

Table 14.3 outlines some suitable specifications for ceiling, floor, and wall finishes within a hotel development with reasonable to good levels of control for reverberation.

Table 14.3 Recommended floor, wall, and ceiling finishes by material or absorption coefficient α_w (hotels)

Room	Floor α_w	Ceiling finish α_w	Wall α_w
Corridors	0.3 carpet (avoid laminate or tile finishes)	0.8 ceiling if floor is carpeted 0.9 if floor is vinyl finish	Plaster or gypsum board
Bars	0.3 carpet preferred, can vary	0.8 ceiling if floor is carpeted 0.9 if floor is vinyl, timber, or tile	Plaster or gypsum board
Restaurants	0.3 carpet preferred, can vary	0.8 ceiling if floor is carpeted 0.9 if floor is vinyl, timber, or tile	Plaster or gypsum board
Reception areas	0.3 carpet preferred, can vary	0.8 ceiling if floor is carpeted 0.9 if floor is vinyl, timber, or tile	Plaster or gypsum board
Meeting rooms (small) <5	0.3 carpet	0.8 over 50 percent of ceiling	0.8 over 25 percent of wall area
Meeting room (large) >5–20	0.3 carpet	0.8 over 50 percent of ceiling	0.8 over 25 percent of wall area
Fitness room	0.3 non-slip carpet or carpet tile	0.8 absorptive ceiling below plasterboard or structural ceiling	Plaster or gypsum board
Swimming pool	Unrated, tile	0.6 spray finish	0.4 slotted block or unpainted block

Further reading

Steel, C. (2010) *Acoustic design assessment. Hotel development.* Unpublished technical report. Edinburgh: RMP Acoustics.

Design tables and equations

A.1 Frequency and wavelength of sound

THE SPEED OF SOUND, the frequency of sound, and the wavelength of sound are fundamentally linked. By knowing two factors, it is possible to determine the third. The speed of sound is generally taken as a constant (c):

$$c = \frac{f}{\lambda}$$

Eq. A.1

c = Speed of sound (343 meters per second)
f = frequency (Hz)
λ = wavelength (m)

Table A.1 shows 1/3 octave bands with corresponding wavelengths.

Table A.1 **Wavelength of sound waves at 1/3 octave bands given in meters and feet**

Frequency (Hz)	100	125	160	200	250	315	400	500	630
Wavelength (m)	3.43	2.74	2.14	1.72	1.37	1.09	0.86	0.69	0.54
Wavelength (ft)	11.25	9	7.03	5.63	4.5	3.57	2.81	2.25	1.79
Frequency (Hz)	800	1000	1250	1600	2000	2500	3150	4000	5000
Wavelength (m)	0.43	0.34	0.27	0.21	0.17	0.14	0.11	0.09	0.07
Wavelength (ft)	1.41	1.13	0.9	0.7	0.56	0.45	0.36	0.35	0.28

A.2 Sound pressure and sound power

THE LEVEL OF NOISE created by a source can either be expressed as a sound power level (SWL) or a sound pressure level (SPL). The term "SWL" is used for sound power levels because they are expressed in units of watts. The term

"SPL" is used for sound pressure levels because they are expressed in units of Pascals. They both express the same thing: how much energy is used to create a sound wave.

Because the scale over which sound power and sound pressure are measured is so vast (they cover the noise created by the tiny release of energy from a bee's wing to massive release of energy from a Saturn 5 rocket or volcanic eruption), they are both referenced against the logarithmic scale. Hence they are both described in dB. This can lead to confusion as noise levels for mechanical equipment are often given as sound power levels (e.g. L_{WA} 89 dB). A simple rule of thumb is that sound power levels are independent of distance, while sound pressure levels are given at a distance from the sound source (e.g., L_{Aeq} 69 dB @ 5 m would be a sound pressure level). Sound power levels can be converted to sound pressure levels.

$$L_p = L_w - 20\log r - 8 \qquad\qquad Eq.\ A.2$$

L_p = Sound pressure level
L_w = Sound power level
r = distance from source to the assessment position (m)

This equation assumes a point source in a hemispherical condition e.g., mechanical equipment fixed on a roof.

A.2.1 Adding sound levels

Because sound is measured on a logarithmic scale, adding together sound levels is not a linear process (i.e. 3 dB + 3 dB *does not* = 6 dB). To add together a number of sound sources in a room or outside a building, such as mechanical equipment, they must be logarithmically summed:

$$L_t = 10\log\left[10^{\frac{L_1}{10}} + 10^{\frac{L_2}{10}} + \ldots\ldots 10^{\frac{L_n}{10}}\right] \qquad\qquad Eq.\ A.3$$

L_t = Total noise level from multiple sources (dB)
L_n = Level of each noise source (dB)

Once the difference between two noise levels is greater than 10 dB, there is no appreciable increase in the overall noise level. Table A.2 outlines

Table A.2 **Adding dB**

Difference in dB between two sound levels	Level in dB to be added to the louder sound source
0–1	3
2–3	2
4–9	1
10 or greater	0

how many dB should be added to a higher noise level dependent on the difference between the two noise levels.

Table A.2 can be used as a simplistic method of adding noise levels, as shown in the example below:

Noise source 1 – 81 dB
Noise source 2 – 84 dB
Noise source 3 – 54 dB
Noise source 4 – 83 dB

Start by discounting any level which is –10 dB below any of the other sources (i.e., noise source 3). Next add the two loudest levels together (noise sources 2 and 4) using Table A.2. Then add the sum of these two levels to the remaining source (noise source 1).

Equipment 1 – 81 dB		81 dB	
Equipment 2 – 84 dB	84 dB		88 dB
Equipment 3 – ~~54 dB~~		87 dB	
Equipment 4 – 83 dB	83 dB		

A.2.2 Averaging sound levels

If you have several measurements of a single noise source taken over a number of separate surveys and find that the noise level varies, you may wish to average these noise levels. Because sound is measured on a decibel scale we *cannot* arithmetically average these levels and they must be logarithmically averaged.

$$L_{av} = \left[\frac{10^{\frac{L_1}{10}} + 10^{\frac{L_2}{10}} + \ldots\ldots 10^{\frac{L_n}{10}}}{n} \right]$$

$\qquad\qquad\qquad\qquad\qquad\qquad\qquad$ Eq. A.4

L_{av} = average noise level (dB)
L_n = the individual noise measurement (dB)
n = number of measurements taken on the single noise source

A.2.3 Sound propagation

For a point source (noise from a small single object), sound pressure will reduce at –6 dB for every doubling of distance. For a line source (such as a road or railway line), sound pressure will reduce at –3 dB for every doubling of distance. This is used to determine noise levels at a proposed building façade when the noise source has been measured at a position closer than the proposed façade.

$Distance\ attenuation\ (point\ source) = 20log(\frac{r_1}{r_2})$ $\qquad$ Eq. A.5

$Distance\ attenuation\ (line\ source) = 10log(\frac{r_1}{r_2})$ $\qquad$ Eq. A.6

r_1 = the distance at which the sound was measured (m)
r_2 = the distance at which the sound is to be predicted (m)

A.2.4 Attenuation from barriers

The performance of an acoustic barrier can be determined by knowing the differences in the path length that a sound wave would have to travel to get over the barrier in relation to how far it would have to travel if the barrier were not there.

$A_{barrier} \approx 10log(3 \pm 20N)$ $\qquad\qquad\qquad\qquad$ Eq. A.7

$\qquad$ So long as $N > –0.05$ then $N = 2\delta/\lambda$
$\qquad$ λ is the frequency (Hz)
$\qquad$ δ is the path difference defined in Figure A.1 (m)

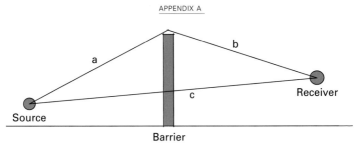

A.1 Attenuation of sound by a barrier

$$a + b - c = \delta \; (path\; difference) \qquad\qquad Eq.\; A.8$$

A.3 Room acoustics

A.3.1 Noise break-in

The difference in noise levels from outside to inside a building can be predicted if the sound reduction or sound transmission index of a façade is known. The predicted level is dependent on understanding the level of absorption within the room:

$$D = R - 10 log \; \frac{S}{A} - 6 \; db \qquad\qquad Eq.\; A.9$$

D = difference in noise level $L_{(outside)}$ and $L_{(inside)}$
R = sound reduction index of the building façade (dB)
S = surface area of the façade (m²)
A = total absorption within the room

A.3.2 Noise break-out

It is also possible to determine the level of noise breaking out from a room by knowing the properties of the façade and how far away the noise receiver position is:

$$D = R - 10 log \; S + 14 + 20 log \; r \qquad\qquad Eq.\; A.10$$

D = difference in noise level $L_{(outside)}$ and $L_{(inside)}$
R = sound reduction index of the building façade (dB)

S = *surface area of the façade (m^2)*
r = *distance from the façade to the assessment position (m)*

When constructing an enclosure around mechanical equipment, a more simplistic noise break-out calculation can be used to determine the insertion loss of an enclosure:

$$L_{(outside)} = L_{(inside)} - R - 6 \qquad\qquad Eq.\ A.11$$

R = *sound reduction index of the enclosure (dB)*

A.3.3 Sound transmission

It is possible to predict the level of sound transmission from one room to another by knowing the insulation properties of the partition, the area of the receiving room, and the amount of acoustic absorption within the receiving room:

$$L_{(receiving\ room)} = L_{(source\ room)} - R + 10log(\frac{S}{A}) \qquad\qquad Eq.\ A.12$$

$L_{(receiving\ room)}$ = *noise level in the receiving room (dB)*
$L_{(source\ room)}$ = *noise level in the source room (dB)*

R = *sound reduction of the partition (dB) defined as the relationship between the transmitted sound and incident sound so that $R = 10log(1/t)$ where $t = \frac{transmitted\ sound}{incident\ sound}$ or the measured reduction.*

S = *surface area of the partition separating the two rooms (m^2)*
A = *absorption in the receiving room (m^2)*

A.3.4 The resonance frequency of a single leaf partition

Where the stiffness of a partition is no longer the dominant factor in controlling sound transmission, a resonance dip will occur, resulting in a loss of performance. This is where the dimensions of a partition along with its material dictate its fundamental resonance, a frequency at which the panel will most easily vibrates. The resonance frequency of a panel can be defined from:

$$f = \frac{m}{2}\sqrt{\frac{E}{12\rho}}\left[\frac{1}{a^2} + \frac{1}{b^2}\right] \qquad\qquad Eq.\ A.13$$

f = *fundamental resonance, resonance frequency (Hz)*
t = *panel thickness (m)*
a = *length of the panel (m)*
b = *height of the panel (m)*
ρ = *density (kg/m³) of panel*
E = *Young's modulus (Pa)*

The density and Young's modulus of some common materials are given in Table A.3.

A.3.5 The natural frequency of a twin leaf partition

Just as it is possible to predict the resonance frequency of a single leaf partition, it is also possible to predict the natural frequency of a twin leaf partition. This can be defined as:

$$f = 60 \sqrt{\left[(m_1 + m_2)/(m_2 m_2 d)\right]}$$ Eq. A.14

f = *natural frequency of the twin leaf partition (Hz)*
m_1 = *mass of the first panel (kg/m²)*
m_2 = *mass of the second panel (kg/m²)*
d = *depth of the cavity (m)*

A.3.6 Mass law equation for separating partitions

The mass of a structure is the dominant factor in controlling sound transmission between the fundamental resonance frequency and coincidence frequency of a partition. The acoustic performance of a mass-controlled

Table A.3 Young's modulus and density of materials

Material	Young's modulus (Pa)	Density (kg/m³)
Aluminum	7×10^{10}	2700
Brick	1.6×10^{10}	1900
Concrete	2.4×10^{10}	2300
Chipboard	1.34×10^{9}	695
Glass	4×10^{10}	2500
OSB	3.5×10^{9}	640
Plasterboard	1.9×10^{9}	750
Plywood	4.3×10^{9}	580

partition improves as the frequency of the sound acting upon it increases. It is therefore possible to make a simple determination of the level of acoustic insulation of a wall or floor for each frequency simply by knowing the mass of the structure.

$$Sound\ reduction = 20log(Mf) - 47 \qquad\qquad Eq.\ A.15$$

$M = mass\ (kg/m^2)$
$f = frequency\ (Hz)$

A.3.7 Critical frequency of a partition

The critical frequency limits the mass-controlled region and occurs where the wavelength of the incident-grazing sound wave is equal to the surface-bending wavelength of a material. The critical frequency can be calculated using the following equation:

$$F_c = \frac{c^2}{1.8hC_L}\ (Hz) \qquad\qquad Eq.\ A.16$$

$F_c = critical\ frequency\ (Hz)$
$c = speed\ of\ sound\ in\ air\ (m/s)$
$C_L = longitudinal\ velocity\ of\ sound\ in\ the\ partition\ (m/s)$, defined as the square root of Young's modulus of elasticity divided by the density of the material (shown in Table A.3).

A.3.8 Composite partitions or façades levels

It is often the case that partitions are made up of several elements (e.g., a brick wall with a door in it or a concrete façade with a window). By knowing the sound reduction index of each element and its surface area, it is possible to determine composite insulation value of the partition:

$$R_{comp} = 10log_{10}\ \frac{S_1 + S_2 + \ldots\ldots\ldots\ldots S_n dB}{10^{\frac{R_1}{10}} \times S_1 + 10^{\frac{R_2}{10}} \times S_1 + 10^{\frac{R_n}{10}} \times S_n} \qquad Eq.\ A.17$$

$R_{comp} = composite\ sound\ reduction\ index\ of\ the\ whole\ wall\ or\ façade\ (dB)$
$S = surface\ area\ of\ a\ partition\ element\ in\ (m^2)$
$R_n = sound\ reduction\ index\ of\ an\ element\ of\ the\ façade\ (window,\ door,\ etc.)\ (dB)$

A.3.9 Absorption

The amount of acoustic absorption within a room is useful in calculating the total noise level within a space, as it quantifies how much sound is absorbed by things like surface finishes and even furniture. Appendix B details the absorption coefficient (α) of some common materials. By knowing the absorption coefficient of each surface in a room and its area, we can determine the absorption within a room:

$$A = S\,\alpha \qquad\qquad Eq.\ A.18$$

A = absorption (total absorption of a surface)
S = surface area of the material being assessed (m^2)
α = absorption coefficient of a material (see Appendix B) equal to the sound energy not reflected from a material divided by the sound energy acting upon it

The total absorption within a room can be calculated by summing the area and absorption coefficients of each material or surface

$$A_{room} = S_1\,\alpha_1 + S_2\,\alpha_2 + \ldots\ldots\ldots\ S_n\,\alpha_n \qquad\qquad Eq.\ A.19$$

A_{room} = total absorption within the room
S_n = surface area of each material being assessed (m^2)
α = absorption coefficient of each material being assessed

A.3.10 Panel absorbers

For acoustically absorptive panels the mass of the panel, the distance the panel is set out from the wall or ceiling, and the frequency of the sound waves which cause it to sympathetically vibrate are linked (Figure A.2). By knowing two factors, it is possible to determine the third. This would allow you to determine how much space may be lost in a room as a result of having to set an acoustically absorptive panel a set distance from a wall in order to resolve a reverberation issue at a particular frequency.

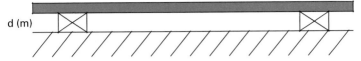

A.2 Panel absorber

$$f = \frac{60}{\sqrt{md}}$$

Eq. A.20

f = frequency (Hz)
m = mass of the panel (kg)
d = distance of panel from wall or ceiling (m)

Table A.4 outlines cavity depths for panels with a mass of 2.5 kg, 5 kg, and 10 kg respectively, depending on frequency.

Panel absorbers are good at controlling reverberant sound at low frequencies partly because the cavity depths become impractically small above 250 Hz.

A.3.11 Cavity absorbers

Cavity absorbers, also known as Helmholtz resonators, are also intended for frequency-specific absorption. They are most useful at absorbing sound at the resonance frequency. This frequency is defined by the air volume inside the resonator as well as the dimensions of the opening (or neck). Figure A.3 and Eq. A.21 explain the relationship between these parameters and the resonance frequency.

Table A.4 **Cavity depths in mm to achieve panel absorption for panels of three common weights**

Frequency (Hz)	Cavity depth by 1/3 octave band							
	100	125	160	200	250	315	400	500
2.5kg/m² panel	144 mm	92 mm	56 mm	36 mm	23 mm	14 mm	9 mm	5 mm
5kg/m² panel	72 mm	46 mm	28 mm	18 mm	11 mm	7 mm	5 mm	3 mm
10kg/m² panel	36 mm	23 mm	14 mm	9 mm	6 mm	4 mm	2 mm	1 mm

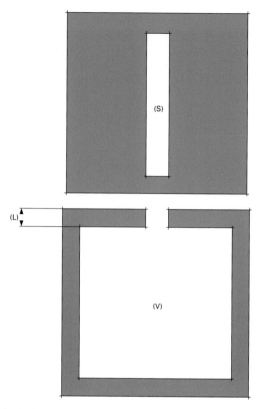

A.3 Cavity absorber/resonator

$$f = c/2\pi \sqrt{\frac{S}{LV}}$$

Eq. A.21

f = *resonance frequency (Hz)*
c = *speed of sound*
S = *cross-sectional area of the neck* (m^2)
L = *length of the neck* (m)
V = *volume of the cavity* (m^3)

A.3.12 Reverberation time

Calculation of the reverberation is useful in determining how suitable a room is likely to be for its purpose. Table B.1 details optimum reverberation times for particular spaces, and this can be predicted prior to construction to ensure that a suitable environment will be designed using the following equations:

Sabine equation – more accurate for live rooms with small amounts of absorption and lots of reflections

$$T = \frac{0.16V}{A} \qquad\qquad Eq.\ A.22$$

T = reverberation time within the room (s)
V = volume of the room (m^3)
A = total absorption within the room (see Eq. A.19)

Norris–<u>Eyring equation</u> – more accurate for dead rooms with high-level absorption and fewer reflections

$$T = \frac{0.16V}{-S\ \ln(1-\alpha_{average})} \qquad\qquad Eq.\ A.23$$

T = reverberation time within the room (s)
S = surface area of the room (m^2)
$\alpha_{average}$ = average absorption coefficient of all surfaces and materials within the room

The average absorption of a room can be calculated by using the following equation:

$$A_{average} = \frac{S_1\alpha_1 + S_2\alpha_2 + \ldots\ldots\ldots\ldots S_n\alpha_n}{S_{total}} \qquad\qquad Eq.\ A.24$$

$A_{average}$ = average absorption within a room
S_n = surface area of a particular material or surface within the room (m^2)
α_n = absorption coefficient of the material or surface
S_{total} = total surface area of the room (m^2)

A.3.13 Optimum reverberation times

These levels can also be predicted using the Stevens and Bates formula:

$$T = r(0.0118(V^{\frac{1}{3}})+0.1070) \qquad \text{Eq. A.25}$$

$T = $ reverberation time (s)

$r = $ room factor dependent on preferred use, therefore:

$r = 4$; for speech
$r = 5$; for orchestral music
$r = 6$; for choral/organ music

$V = $ volume of room (m³)

Note: This is the optimum reverberation time at 500 Hz. Add 30 percent to the result to determine optimum at 125 Hz. Reduce the result by 20 percent to determine the optimum at 4 kHz.

A.3.14 Speech clarity, C50

The equation to calculate C50 for a room, proposed by L. G. Marshall, is a weighted average of the values at the octave band frequencies between 500 Hz and 4 kHz, the range at which we find speech:

$$C50 = 0.15\,C50_{500} + 0.25\,C50_{1K} + 0.35\,C50_{2K} + 0.25\,C50_{4K}; \text{ in dB} \quad \text{Eq. A.26}$$

A.3.15 Music clarity, C80

The equation to calculate C80 for a room, proposed by L. Beranek, is an average of the values at the octave band frequencies between 500 Hz and 2 kHz:

$$C80 = \frac{C80_{500} + C80_{1K} + C80_{2K}}{3} \text{ in dB} \qquad \text{Eq. A.27}$$

Further reading

Hopkins, C. (2008) Sound insulation: Theory into practice. London: Routledge.
Sharland, I. (1972) Woods practical guide to noise control. Colchester, UK: Woods.

appendix B

Performance criteria

INFORMATION PROVIDED IN THIS APPENDIX sets good to reasonable standards for:

■ Ambient noise associated with sound from sources outside the room under consideration. These are set as average noise level (L_{Aeq}). No time parameter has been set, but a minimum measurement period would be one hour. Daytime periods are assumed to be 7:00AM to 11:00PM; nighttime periods are assumed to be 11:00PM to 7:00AM.

■ The control of noise within a room from mechanical equipment either associated with the building or with an adjoining building/activity. These are defined as Noise Criteria (popular in North America) or Noise Ratings (popular in Europe) and are based on the performance levels across a frequency range. Table 6.3 details the most common rating curves.

■ The control of echoes within a room defined as the maximum possible reverberation time in seconds.

■ Impact sound insulation from floors above a room, in order to provide adequate control of noise from footfall. This is shown as the Field Impact Insulation Class (FIIC) or the single figure weighted Sound Transmission Level ($L'_{nT,w}$), which are popular in North America and Europe respectively.

■ Airborne sound insulation performance requirements for a range of room adjacencies by building type. These are presented as laboratory performance standards (STC for North America, and R_w for Europe). To determine on-site performance levels, these values can be adjusted by applying the rules of thumb outlined in Chapter 6 (Section 6.4.3).

■ Airborne sound insulation performance requirements for a range of doors dependent on room type. Again these are displayed as laboratory performance levels (STC/R_w).

Table B.1 Recommended acoustic performance levels by room type

Room type	Upper ambient noise level (L_{Aeq}) dB		Upper NRC/NR noise level	Maximum reverberation time (sec)	Minimum FIIC dB	Maximum $L'_{nT,w}$ dB
	Day	Night	Day or night			
		HOTELS				
		Front of house				
Banqueting/function hall	35	35	35	0.8	55	55
Bar	40	40	35	1	55	55
Corridor	45	40	<35–40	1.5	n/a	n/a
Fitness center	<40–45	40–45	<35–40	1	55	55
Foyer/lobby	<35–45	35–45	<35–40	1.5		
Guestroom	<30–45	<25–35	<20–30	0.6	65	45
Guestroom bathroom	50	45	<40–45	1	60	50
Lounge	40	40	<30–35	1	55	55
Meeting room	<35–40	<35–40	<30–35	0.6	55	55
Reception	40	40	35	1.5	55	55
Restaurant	45	45	<35–40	1	55	55
Shop	<50–55	<50–55	<40–45	<0.8–1.0	55	55
Spa	<30–40	<30–40	<25–35	1.5	55	55
Stair	40	40	35		n/a	n/a
Toilet/restroom	50	50	<35–45	1.5	n/a	n/a

Back of house

Kitchen	<45–50	<45–50	<40–45	1.5	50	60
Laundry	<45–50	<45–50	<40–45	1.5	n/a	n/a
Office	<35–40	<35–40	<30–40	1	50	60
Service area	<45–50	<45–50	<40–45	1.5	n/a	n/a
Staff room	<40–45	<40–45	<40–45	1	50	60

OFFICES

Atrium/foyer	45	45	40	1.5	45	65
Board room	<35–40	<35–40	<30–35	0.8	45	65
Cafeteria	45	45	40	1	45	65
Computer server room	80	80	75	–	n/a	n/a
Confidential/interview meeting room	<35–40	<35–40	<30–35	<0.6–0.9	45	65
Informal meeting/telephone room	<35–45	<35–45	<30–40	1	45	65
Large meeting >5–20 people	<35–40	<35–40	<30–35	0.8	45	65
Large office >8–15 people	<35–45	<35–45	<30–40	1	45	65
Lecture room <50 people	<35–40	<35–40	<30–35	1	45	65
Lecture room >50 people	<35–40	<35–40	<30–35	0.8	45	65
Open-plan interactive working	<40–50	<40–50	<35–45	1.0*	45	65
Open-plan quiet working	<40–50	<40–50	<35–45	1.0*	45	65
Plant room	80	80	75	–	n/a	n/a
Reception	<35–45	<35–45	<30–40	1	45	65
Seminar room	<35–45	<35–45	<25–30	0.8	45	65
Single/executive office	<35–45	<35–45	<30–40	<0.6–0.8	45	65
Small meeting <5 people	<35–40	<35–40	<30–35	0.8	45	65
Small office 2–8 people	<35–45	<35–45	<30–45	0.5	45	65

Table B.1 continued

Room type	Upper ambient noise level (L_{Aeq}) dB		Upper NRC/NR noise level	Maximum reverberation time (sec)	Minimum FIIC dB	Maximum $L'_{nT,w}$ dB
	Day	Night	Day or night			
Staff room/staff kitchen	<35–45	<35–45	<30–40	1	45	65
Tele-/videoconferencing room	<25–35	<25–35	20	0.8	45	65
Toilets/changing room	50	50	45	1.5	45	65
EDUCATIONAL						
Teaching space						
Art rooms	40	n/a	35	0.8	50	60
Elementary/primary school classroom	35	n/a	30	0.6	50	60
General classroom/tutorial room	35	n/a	30	0.8	50	60
Kindergarten/nursery school room	35	n/a	30	0.6	50	60
Language labs	35	n/a		0.8	50	60
Large lecture room > 50 students	35	n/a	30	1	50	60
Open-plan breakout areas	40	n/a	35	1.2	50	60
Open-plan teaching space	40	n/a	35	0.5	50	60
Science laboratories	40	n/a	35	0.8	50	60
Small lecture room < 50 students	35	n/a	30	0.8	50	60
Special needs teaching space	30	n/a	25	125 Hz–2 kHz –0.4/0.6 at all	55	55

				other octave band frequencies		
Study room (individual or withdrawn study)	40	n/a	35	0.8	50	60
Teaching kitchens, electronics, textile, ICT	40	n/a	35	0.8	50	60
Resource space						
Assembly halls/Multipurpose halls	35	n/a	30	<0.8–1.2	50	60
Atria/social interaction space	45	n/a	40	1.5	45	65
Dining rooms	45	n/a	40	1	45	65
Drama studio	35	n/a	30	1	50	60
Library quiet space	40	n/a	35	1	50	60
Library resource space	40	n/a	35	1	50	60
Meeting/Interview/counseling	40	n/a	35	0.8	50	60
Workshops (metal/woodworking/machine)	40	n/a	35	0.8 (if purely vocational, e.g., practical work only relax to 1.5)	50	
Musical space						
Music ensemble room	35	n/a	30	<0.6–1.2	55	55
Music group practice room >30m³	35	n/a	30	0.8	55	55
Music group practice room <30m³	35	n/a	30	0.6	55	55
Music performance/recital room	35	n/a	30	<1.0–1.5	55	55
Music room (elementary/primary)	35	n/a	30	1	50	60
Music room (middle/high/secondary)	35	n/a	30	1	55	55
Recording studio	35	n/a	30	<0.6–1.2	55	55
Recording studio control room	35	n/a	30	0.5	55	55

Table B.1 continued

Room type	Upper ambient noise level (L_{Aeq}) dB		Upper NRC/NR noise level	Maximum reverberation time (sec)	Minimum FIIC dB	Maximum $L'_{nT,w}$ dB
	Day	Night	Day or night			
Sports facilities						
Dance studio	40	n/a	35	1.2	50	60
Gymnasium	40	n/a	35	1.5	50	60
Sports halls	40	n/a	35	2	50	60
Swimming pools	50	n/a	45	2	45	65
Ancillary space						
Changing rooms	50	n/a	45	1.5	45	65
Corridors/stairwells/cloakrooms	45	n/a	40	Note 4	45	65
Kitchens	50	n/a	45	1	45	65
Offices/medical rooms/staff rooms	45	n/a	40	1	45	65
Toilets/showers	50	n/a	45	1.5	45	65
HEALTHCARE						
Patient care/clinical						
Birthing room	45	n/a	40	See Section 8.2.3	45	65
Children and older people (multi–bed)	45	35	30	See Section 8.2.3	45	65
Children and older people (single bed)	40	35	30	See Section 8.2.3	45	65
Consulting room	40	n/a	35	See Section 8.2.3	45	65

Counseling/bereavement room	40	n/a	35	See Section 8.2.3	45	65
En suite toilets (non cubicles)	45	n/a	40	See Section 8.2.3	45	65
Examination room	40	n/a	35	See Section 8.2.3	45	65
Medical interview room	40	n/a	35	See Section 8.2.3	45	65
Multi-faith/chapel	40	n/a	35	See Section 8.2.3	45	65
Nurseries	40	35	30	See Section 8.2.3	45	65
Operating theater suite	40	n/a	40 (50 Laminar flow)	See Section 8.2.3	45	65
Rest room	45	35	30	See Section 8.2.3	45	65
Single bed/on-call room	40	35	30	See Section 8.2.3	45	65
Snoezelen/multisensory room	30	n/a	25	See Section 8.2.3	45	65
Speech and language therapy	30	n/a	25	See Section 8.2.3	45	65
Treatment room	40	n/a	35	See Section 8.2.3	45	65
Administration/staff areas						
Boardroom	35	n/a	30	See Section 8.2.3	45	65
Clean utility	55	n/a	40	See Section 8.2.3	45	65
Dirty utility/sluice	55	n/a	40	See Section 8.2.3	45	65
Laboratories	45	n/a	40	See Section 8.2.3	45	65
Large meeting room (>35m^2)	35	n/a	30	See Section 8.2.3	45	65
Large training/seminar (>35m^2)	35	n/a	30	See Section 8.2.3	45	65
Library/archiving room	40	n/a	35	See Section 8.2.3	45	65
Locker/changing room	55	n/a	40	See Section 8.2.3	45	65
Main kitchen	55	n/a	50 (55 at extract hood)	See Section 8.2.3	45	65
Medical lecture theater	35	n/a	30	See Section 8.2.3	45	65
Medical storeroom	n/a	n/a	n/a	See Section 8.2.3	45	65
Multi-person office (2–4 people)	40	n/a	40	See Section 8.2.3	45	65

Table B.1 continued

Room type	Upper ambient noise level (L_{Aeq}) dB		Upper NRC/NR noise level	Maximum reverberation time (sec)	Minimum FIIC dB	Maximum $L'_{nT,w}$ dB
	Day	Night	Day or night			
Open-plan office (>5 people)	45	n/a	40	See Section 8.2.3	45	65
Single-person office	40	n/a	35	See Section 8.2.3	45	65
Small meeting room (<35m²)	40	n/a	35	See Section 8.2.3	45	65
Small training/seminar(<35m²)	40	n/a	35	See Section 8.2.3	45	65
Ward kitchen, pantry	50	n/a	40	See Section 8.2.3	45	65
Ancillary space						
Atrium	55	n/a	40	See Section 8.2.3	45	65
Corridor (no door)	55	n/a	40	See Section 8.2.3	45	65
Dining	50	n/a	40	See Section 8.2.3	45	65
Public/staff toilets (non cubicles)	55	n/a	45	See Section 8.2.3	45	65
Waiting (large >20 people)	50	n/a	40	See Section 8.2.3	45	65
Waiting (small <20 people)	50	n/a	40	See Section 8.2.3	45	65
COMMERCIAL						
Back of house	<40–50	<40–50	<35–45	1.2	n/a	n/a
Bar/nightclub	<40–45	<40–45	<35–40	1	55	55
Café	45	45	35	1	45	65
Cinema auditorium (shell)	30	30	25(L_{Amax})	n/a	60	50

Cinema concession area (shell)	45	45	40 ($L_{A_{max}}$)	n/a	45	65
Commercial kitchen	<45–50	<45–50	<40–45	1.5	50	60
Dentist	35	35	25	As per Section 8.2.3	45	65
Department store/supermarket	50	50	45	1.5	n/a	n/a
Exhibition space/gallery	<40–45	<40–45	<35–40	1.2	45	65
Fitness center	<40–45	<40–45	<35–40	1	55	55
Hairdresser	40	40	35	1	45	65
Pharmacy/chemist	40	40	35	0.8	45	65
Restaurant	45	45	<35–40	1	55	55
Shopping mall concourse	45	45	40	1.5	45	65
Small shop/retail unit	50	50	45	1	55	55
Spa	<30–40	<30–40	<25–35	<0.8–1.0	55	55
Swimming pools	50	n/a	45	2	45	65
Toilets/showers	50	n/a	45	1.5	45	65
Underground parking	<60–70	<60–70	<55–65			
CIVIC/GOVERNMENTAL						
Church/religious (serious liturgical music)	30	30	20	Note 2	45	65
Church/religious (small)	35	35	25	Note 2	45	65
Committee rooms	40	40	35	0.8–1.0	45	65
Concert halls	<25–30	<25–30	<20–25	Note 2	50	60
Control centers	LA90 30–35	LA90 30–35	<25–30	<0.4–0.75	50	60
Court rooms	<30–40	<30–40	25	<0.6–1.0 (125 Hz–2 kHz)	50	60
Custody areas	45	45	40	1	45	65

Table B.1 continued

Room type	Upper ambient noise level (L_{Aeq}) dB		Upper NRC/NR noise level	Maximum reverberation time (sec)	Minimum FIIC dB	Maximum $L'_{nT,w}$ dB
	Day	Night	Day or night			
Interview rooms (for recording)	35	35	30	0.3	50	60
Library	<40–50	<40–50	<35–45	0.6	50	60
Magistrates/judge retiring, judge's chambers	40	40	35	0.6	45	65
Museum	<40–50	<40–50	<35–45	1.0–1–5	45	65
Prison cell	30	30	25	1	45	65
Public baths/swimming pools	<50–55	<50–55	<45–50	2	45	65
Theater	<25–30	<25–30	<20–25	Note 2	50	60
Toilets	50	50	45	1.5	45	65
Videoconferencing	<25–35	<25–35	20	0.8	45	65
Washrooms	50	50	45	1.5	45	65
INDUSTRIAL						
Automotive repair	65	65	65	1.8	n/a	n/a
Canteen	<50–55	<50–55	<45–50	1	45	65
Commercial laboratories	<45–55	<45–55	<40–50	0.8	50	60
Garages	<65–75	<65–75	<45–65	n/a	n/a	n/a
Heavy engineering	<70–80	<70–80	<55–75	n/a	n/a	n/a
Industrial workshop	<65–70	<65–70	<65–70	2	n/a	n/a

Light engineering	<65–75	<65–75	n/a	<45–65	n/a	n/a
Loading bays	<60–75	<60–75	n/a	<55–60	n/a	n/a
Rest rooms	<40–45	<40–45	1	<40–45	45	65
Warehouses	<65–75	<65–75	n/a	<45–65	n/a	n/a
Workshops	<50–60	<50–60	2	<60–70	n/a	n/a
DOMESTIC						
Bedrooms	<35	<30	0.6	<20–25	Note 3	Note 3
Living rooms	<40	<30	0.8	<25–35	Note 3	Note 3

Table B.2 Suitable laboratory performance levels for separating partitions within a hotel development – STC/R_w (dB)

Room types	Guest room	Plant room	Other guest room bathroom	Meeting room	Corridor (no door)	Bar	Reception	Restaurant	Stair	Banqueting/function hall	Shop	Lounge	Public toilet/restroom	Spa	Fitness center	Kitchen	Office	Staff room	Laundry
Guestroom	*	70	*	65	65	65	55	65	65	75	60	65	65	65	65	70	65	65	70
Plant room		n/a	*	65	55	60	60	65	55	60	60	60	45	60	60	n/a	60	55	n/a
Other guest room bathroom			*	*	*	*	*	*	*	*	*	*	*	*	*	*	*	*	*
Meeting room				55	55	60	55	60	55	60	55	55	50	60	60	65	55	60	65
Corridor (no door)					n/a	50	45	50	n/a	50	45	45	40	50	50	55	50	50	55
Bar						50	50	50	45	50	50	50	40	55	55	50	55	50	55
Reception							n/a	50	45	55	50	50	45	55	55	55	50	50	55
Restaurant								50	45	50	50	50	40	50	50	45	50	50	55
Stair									n/a	50	45	45	40	55	55	45	50	45	45
Banqueting/function hall										50	50	50	40	50	50	50	50	50	55
Shop											50	50	40	55	55	50	50	45	50
Lounge												50	40	45	50	55	45	50	55
Public toilet/restroom													40	55	55	55	50	50	45
Spa														55	50	55	50	50	55
Fitness center															50	45	50	50	55
Kitchen																45	50	45	n/a
Office																	50	50	60
Staff room																		45	50
Laundry																			n/a

Table B.3 Suitable laboratory performance levels for separating partitions within an office development – STC/R_w (dB)

Room types	Reception	Atrium/foyer	Cafeteria	Single/executive office	Confidential/interview meeting room	Board room	Small office 2–8 people	Large office >8–15 people	Open-plan quiet working	Open-plan interactive working	Small meeting <5 people	Large meeting >5–20 people	informal meeting/telephone room	Seminar room	Tele-/video conferencing room	Lecture room <50 people	Lecture room >50 people	Staff room/staff kitchen	Toilets/changing room	Computer server room	Plant room
Reception	37	47	47	53	56	56	47	42	37	37	47	47	47	53	53	53	53	47	42	53	53
Atrium/foyer		37	37	53	56	56	53	53	47	37	47	47	53	53	53	53	53	37	37	37	37
Cafeteria			37	53	56	56	53	53	47	37	53	53	53	53	56	56	56	37	37	37	37
Single/executive office				47	56	56	56	56	53	56	53	53	53	53	56	56	53	53	53	53	53
Confidential/interview meeting room					53	56	56	56	56	56	56	56	56	56	56	56	56	56	56	56	56
Board room						53	56	56	56	56	56	56	56	56	56	56	56	56	56	56	56
Small office 2–8 people							47	47	37	53	53	53	42	53	53	53	53	42	47	53	53
Large office >8–15 people								47	47	47	53	53	42	53	53	53	53	42	47	53	53
Open-plan quiet working									47	47	53	53	42	53	53	53	53	42	47	53	53
Open-plan interactive working										47	47	53	42	53	53	56	56	37	42	47	47
Small meeting <5 people											53	53	47	53	53	53	53	47	47	53	53
Large meeting >5–20 people informal meeting/telephone room												53	47	53	53	53	53	47	47	53	53
Seminar room														53	53	53	53	47	47	53	53
Tele-/videoconferencing room															53	56	56	56	53	56	56
Lecture room <50 people																53	53	56	53	56	56
Lecture room >50 people																	53	56	53	56	56
Staff room/staff kitchen																		37	37	37	37
Toilets/changing room																			37	37	37
Computer server room																				37	n/a
Plant room																					n/a

Table B.4 Suitable laboratory performance levels for separating partitions within an

Room types	Workshops (metal/woodworking/machine)	Toilets/showers	Teaching kitchens, electronics, textile, ICT	Swimming pools	Study room (individual or withdrawn study)	Sports halls	Special needs teaching space	Science laboratories	Recording studio control room	Recording studio	Open-plan teaching space
Art rooms	57	52	52	57	52	57	57	52	57	62	52
Assembly halls/multipurpose halls	62	57	57	62	57	62	62	57	62	62	57
Atria/social interaction space	57	52	52	57	52	57	57	52	57	62	57
Changing rooms	52	57	57	52	57	57	62	57	62	62	57
Corridors/stairwells/cloakrooms	57	52	52	57	52	57	57	52	57	62	52
Dance studio	57	57	57	57	57	57	62	57	62	62	57
Dining rooms	57	57	57	57	57	57	62	57	62	62	57
Drama studio	62	57	57	62	57	62	62	57	62	62	57
Elementary/primary school classroom	57	52	52	57	52	57	57	52	57	62	52
General classroom/tutorial room	57	52	52	57	52	57	57	52	57	62	52
Gymnasium	57	57	57	57	57	57	62	57	62	62	57
Kindergarten/nursery school room	57	52	52	57	52	57	57	52	57	62	52
Kitchens	52	57	57	52	57	57	62	57	62	62	57
Language labs	57	52	52	57	52	57	57	52	57	62	52
Lecture room large >50 students	57	52	52	57	52	57	57	52	57	62	52
Lecture room small <50 students	57	52	52	57	52	57	57	52	57	62	52
Library quiet space	52	52	57	57	47	57	52	52	57	62	52
Library resource space	57	52	52	57	52	57	57	52	57	62	52
Meeting/interview/counseling	62	57	62	62	52	62	57	57	62	62	57
Music ensemble room	62	62	62	62	62	62	62	62	62	62	62
Music group practice room >30 m^3	62	62	62	62	62	62	62	62	62	62	62
Music group practice room <30 m^3	62	62	62	62	62	62	62	62	62	62	62
Music performance/recital room	62	62	62	62	62	62	62	62	62	62	62
Music room (elementary/primary)	57	57	57	57	57	57	62	57	62	62	57
Music room (middle/high/secondary)	62	62	62	62	62	62	62	62	62	62	62
Offices/medical rooms/staff rooms	52	52	57	57	47	57	52	52	57	62	52
Open-plan break-out areas	57	52	52	57	52	57	52	52	57	62	52
Open-plan teaching space	57	52	52	57	52	57	57	52	57	62	52
Recording studio	62	62	62	62	62	62	62	62	62	62	
Recording studio control room	62	57	57	62	57	62	62	57	62		
Science laboratories	57	52	52	57	52	57	57	52			
Special needs teaching space	62	57	57	62	52	62	57				
Sports halls	57	57	57	57	57	57					
Study room (individual or withdrawn study)	52	52	57	57	47						
Swimming pools	52	57	57	52							
Teaching kitchens, electronics, textile, ICT	57	52	52								
Toilets/showers	57	52									
Workshops (Metal/woodworking/machine)	52										

educational development – STC/R_w (dB)

Open-plan breakout areas	Offices/medical rooms/staff rooms	Music room (middle/high/secondary)	Music room (elementary/primary)	Music performance/recital room	Music group practice room <30 m^3	Music group practice room >30 m^3	Music ensemble room	MeetingInterview/Counseling	Library resource space	Library Quiet space	Lecture room Small <50 students	Lecture room Large >50 students	Language labs	Kitchens	Kindergarten/nursery school room	Gymnasium	General classroom/tutorial room	Elementary/primary school classroom	Drama studio	Dining rooms	Dance studio	Corridors/stairwells/cloakrooms	Changing rooms	Atria/social interaction space	Assembly halls/multipurpose halls	Art Rooms
52	52	62	57	62	62	62	62	57	52	52	52	52	52	57	52	57	52	52	57	57	57	52	57	52	57	52
57	62	62	62	62	62	62	62	62	57	57	57	57	57	62	57	62	57	57	62	57	57	57	62	57	62	
52	52	62	57	62	62	62	62	57	52	52	52	52	52	57	52	57	52	52	57	57	57	52	57	52		
57	57	62	57	62	62	62	62	62	57	57	57	57	57	52	57	57	57	57	62	57	57	57	52			
52	52	62	57	62	62	62	62	57	52	52	52	52	52	57	52	57	52	52	57	57	57	52				
52	57	62	57	62	62	62	62	62	57	57	57	57	57	57	57	57	57	57	62	57	57					
52	57	62	57	62	62	62	62	62	57	57	57	57	57	57	57	57	57	57	62	57						
57	62	62	62	62	62	62	62	62	57	57	57	57	57	62	57	62	57	57	62							
52	52	62	57	62	62	62	62	57	52	52	52	52	52	57	52	57	52	52								
52	52	62	57	62	62	62	62	57	52	52	52	52	52	57	52	57	52									
52	57	62	57	62	62	62	62	62	57	57	57	57	57	57	57	57										
52	52	62	57	62	62	62	62	57	52	52	52	52	52	57	52											
57	57	62	57	62	62	62	62	62	57	57	57	57	57	52												
52	52	62	57	62	62	62	62	57	52	52	52	52	52													
52	52	62	57	62	62	62	62	57	52	52	52	52														
52	52	62	57	62	62	62	62	57	52	52	52															
52	47	62	57	62	62	62	62	52	52	47																
52	52	62	57	62	62	62	62	57	52																	
57	52	62	62	62	62	62	62	52																		
62	62	62	62	62	62	62	62																			
62	62	62	62	62	62	62																				
62	62	62	62	62	62																					
62	62	62	62	62																						
52	57	62	57																							
62	62	62																								
52	47																									
52																										

Table B.5 Suitable laboratory performance levels for separating partitions within a

Room types	Small meeting room (<35 m²)	Large meeting room (>35 m²)	Boardroom	Open-plan office (>5 people)	Multi-person office (2–4 people)	Single-person office	Library/archiving room	Lecture theater	Small training/seminar(<35 m²)	Large training/seminar (>35 m²)	Locker/changing room	Rest room	Storeroom
Single bed/on-call room	54	54	54	54	54	54	54	54	54	54	54	54	54
Multi-bed room	49	54	54	44	44	49	49	54	49	54	44	49	44
Children and older people (single-bed)	54	54	54	54	54	54	59	59	54	54	49	54	49
Children and older people (multi-bed)	49	54	54	49	49	49	54	54	49	54	44	49	44
Consulting room	54	54	54	54	54	54	54	54	54	54	54	54	54
Examination room	54	54	54	54	54	54	54	54	54	54	54	54	54
Treatment room	54	54	54	54	54	54	54	54	54	54	54	54	54
Counseling/bereavement room	54	54	54	54	54	54	59	59	54	54	54	54	54
Interview room	54	54	54	54	54	54	54	54	54	54	54	54	54
Operating theater suite	54	59	59	59	49	54	54	59	54	59	49	54	49
Nurseries	59	59	59	59	59	59	64*	64*	59	59	54	59	54
Birthing room	59	59	59	59	59	59	64*	64*	59	59	54	59	54
Laboratories	49	54	54	44	44	49	49	54	49	54	44	49	44
Dirty utility/sluice	49	49	54	49	49	49	54	54	49	49	44	49	n/a
Clean utility	49	49	54	n/a	44	49	44	49	49	49	44	44	n/a
Speech and language therapy	54	54	54	54	54	54	59	59	54	54	54	54	54
Snoezelen/multisensory room	54	59	59	54	54	54	59	59	54	59	54	54	54
Multi-faith/chapel	54	59	59	54	54	54	54	54	54	59	54	54	49
Corridor (no door)	49	49	54	n/a	44	49	49	49	49	49	44	44	n/a
Atrium	49	49	54	49	49	49	54	54	49	49	44	49	n/a
Dining	49	49	54	49	49	49	54	54	49	49	44	49	n/a
Toilets (non cubicles)	49	49	54	44	44	49	49	49	49	49	44	44	44
Waiting (large >20 people)	49	49	54	49	49	49	54	54	49	49	44	49	n/a
Waiting (small <20 people)	49	49	54	n/a	44	49	49	49	49	49	44	44	n/a
Toilets (non cubicles)	49	49	54	44	44	49	49	49	49	49	44	44	44
Main kitchen	59	59	59	59	59	59	64*	64*	59	59	54	59	54
Ward kitchen, pantry	49	49	54	n/a	44	49	49	49	49	49	44	44	n/a
Storeroom	49	49	54	n/a	44	49	44	49	49	49	44	44	n/a
Rest room	49	54	54	49	49	49	54	54	49	54	44	49	
Locker/changing room	49	49	54	44	44	49	49	49	49	49	44		
Large training/seminar (>35 m²)	54	54	54	54	54	54	59	59	54	54			
Small training/seminar (<35 m)	49	54	54	49	49	49	54	54	49				
Lecture theater	54	59	59	54	54	54	54	59	59				
Library/archiving room	54	59	59	49	49	54	44						
Single-person office	49	54	54	49	49	49							
Multi-person office (2–4 people)	49	54	54	44	44								
Open-plan office (>5 people)	49	54	54	n/a									
Boardroom	54	54	54										
Large meeting room (>35 m²)	54	54											
Small meeting room (<35 m²)	49												

* Rooms where adjacencies require a minimum of Rw 64 dB should be avoided

healthcare development – STC/R_w (dB)

Ward kitchen, pantry	Main kitchen	Toilets (non cubicles)	Waiting (small <20 people)	Waiting (large >20 people)	Toilets (non cubicles)	Dining	Atrium	Corridor (no door)	Multi-faith/chapel	Snoezelen/multisensory room	Speech and language therapy	Clean utility	Dirty utility/sluice	Laboratories	Birthing room	Nurseries	Operating theater suite	Interview room	Counseling/bereavement room	Treatment room	Examination room	Consulting room	Children and older people (multi-bed)	Children and older people (single-bed)	Multi-bed room	Single bed/on-call room
54	59	54	54	54	54	54	54	54	54	54	54	54	54	54	59	59	54	54	54	54	54	54	54	54	54	54
44	59	44	44	49	44	49	49	44	54	54	54	44	49	44	59	59	49	54	54	54	54	54	49	54	44	
59	59	49	49	49	49	49	49	49	59	59	59	49	49	54	59	59	59	54	54	54	54	54	54			
44	59	44	44	49	44	49	49	44	54	54	54	44	49	49	59	59	59	54	54	54	54	54	49			
54	59	54	54	54	54	54	54	54	54	54	54	54	54	59	59	54	54	54	54	54	54					
54	59	54	54	54	54	54	54	54	54	54	54	54	54	59	59	54	54	54	54	54						
54	59	54	54	54	54	54	54	54	54	59	59	59	54	54	59	59	59	59	54	54						
54	59	54	54	54	54	54	54	54	54	54	54	54	54	59	59	54	54									
49	64*	59	49	54	49	54	54	59	59	59	59	49	54	49	64*	64*	54									
54	59	54	54	54	54	54	54	54	64*	64*	64*	54	54	59	59	59										
54	59	54	54	54	54	54	54	54	64*	64*	64*	54	54	59	59											
44	59	44	44	49	44	49	49	44	54	54	54	44	49	44												
n/a	54	44	n/a	n/a	44	n/a	n/a	n/a	54	54	54	n/a	n/a													
n/a	54	44	n/a	n/a	44	n/a	n/a	n/a	49	54	54	n/a														
54	54	54	54	54	54	54	54	54	59	59	59															
54	64*	54	54	54	54	54	54	54	59	59																
49	64*	49	49	54	49	54	54	49	59																	
n/a	54	44	n/a	n/a	44	n/a	n/a	n/a																		
n/a	54	44	n/a	n/a	44	n/a	n/a																			
n/a	54	44	n/a	n/a	44	n/a																				
44	54	44	44	44	44																					
n/a	54	44	n/a	n/a																						
n/a	54	44	n/a																							
44	54	44																								
54	54																									
n/a																										

Notes:

1 The values outlined in the table provide good practice performance standards for unoccupied rooms with regards to ambient noise, noise from mechanical equipment, reverberation times, and impact sound insulation.

2 Suitable reverberation levels for these spaces are dependent on room volume and expected musical type. Eq. A.25 (in Appendix A) can be used to determine suitable optimum reverberation times.

3 Appropriate impact insulation levels for domestic rooms are outlined in Chapter 12.

4 Optimum reverberation times for corridor spaces associated with schools can be defined as providing a minimum area of absorbent material as detailed in Table 7.4.

Table B.6 **Suitable laboratory performance levels for internal doors – STC/R_w dB**

Door location	Suitable performance level STC/R_w (dB)
Hotels	
Bedroom – corridor	35
Interconnecting doors between bedrooms	Double leaf of 35
Lounge	30
Function rooms	30
Offices	
Office	30
Meeting rooms	35
Commercial	
Kitchen	35
Spa	30
Fitness room	30
Restaurant	30
Bar	30
Auditorium to external	45
Auditorium to concession/lobby	45
Concession/corridor to external	40

Door location	Suitable performance level STC/R_w (dB)
Educational	
Serving hatch shutters	18
Interconnecting door (teaching space to teaching space)	35
Operable walls (drama/teaching – hall)	DnT, w 45
Music to music (access via room)	45
Vision panels halls control rooms	45
Music room	35
Control room	35
Drama room	35
Multipurpose room	35
Special needs	35
All other teaching	35
Healthcare	
Ancillary space/office, etc.	30
Treatment/consulting	35
Civic	
Courtroom/judge's chambers/confidential	45
Non-confidential	35
Interview rooms – recording	45

Further reading

ASHRAE (2009) *ASHRAE handbook*. Atlanta, GA: American Society of Heating, Refrigerating and Air-Conditioning Engineers.

British Standards Institution (1999) *Sound insulation and noise reduction for buildings, code of practice*. S8233:1999. London: BSI.

Ministry of Justice (MOJ) (2007) *Courts standards and design guide*. London: Her Majesty's Court Services.

appendix C

Performance specifications

C.1 Absorption

C.2 Insulation

C.1 Absorption

Table C.1 Acoustic absorption performance levels of common branded building products

System type	Manufacturer	Product name	NRC	ɑW	Absorption class	Comment
Ceilings	Armstrong	Ultima OP	0.95	1	A	Mineral fiber ceiling tile
	RPG	Topperfo Micro Panel	0.95	n/a	A	Perforated wood panel ceiling system
	Ecophon	Super G B	0.9	1	A	Mineral fiber ceiling tile
	Barrisol	A15 Nanoperf	0.83	0.9	A	Perforated PVC sheet system 130 mm ceiling cavity with 40 mm fiber insulation
	Barrisol	A30 Microacoustic	0.9	0.8	B	Perforated PVC sheet system 120 mm ceiling cavity with 40 mm fiber insulation
	Sto	Stosilent A-Tec	0.85	0.86	B	Acoustic plaster on grid ceiling
	Ecophon	Focus A	0.85	0.8	B	Mineral fiber ceiling tile
	Armstrong	Axal Vector	0.8	0.8	B	Perforated metal ceiling tile 200 mm ceiling cavity and 8 mm thick inlay pad
	Idealtec	Ideacustic 8/11/64	0.75	0.8	B	Ridged wood panel (19 percent perforations) with 50 mm cavity and 40 mm mineral fiber
	Ecophon	Gedina E (60 mm)	0.85	0.75	C	Mineral fiber ceiling tile
	Sto	Stosilent Top	0.65	0.63	C	Acoustic plaster on grid ceiling
	Barrisol	A15 Nanoperf	0.62	0.65	C	Perforated PVC sheet system 130 mm ceiling cavity
	Armstrong	Bioguard Acoustic	0.6	0.6	C	Mineral fiber ceiling tile for healthcare applications
	Idealtec	Mi	0.55	0.6	C	Peforated wood (1089 perforations) tile 80 mm cavity 40 mm mineral fiber
	Armstrong	Academy Diploma	0.5	0.55	D	Mineral fiber ceiling tile
	Sto	Sto-Acoustic Plaster	0.45	0.58	D	Plaster finish

Table C.1 Acoustic absorption performance levels of common branded building products (continued)

System type	Manufacturer	Product name	NRC	ἀW	Absorption class	Comment
	Barrisol	A20 Acoperf	0.5	0.5	D	Perforated PVC sheet system 100 mm ceiling cavity
	Idealtec	T32	0.4	0.4	D	Peforated wood (289 perforations) tile 80 mm cavity with 40 mm mineral fiber
	Ecophon	Sombra A/Ga mm	n/a	0.3	D	Mineral fiber ceiling tile
	British Gypsum	Gyptone Plasterboard	0.75	0.75	C	Perforated plasterboard 48 mm cavity with 50 mm mineral fiber quilt
	Lafarge	GTEC Pregybel C10 No.8	n/a	0.6	C	Perforated plasterboard with 300 mm cavity
	Knauf Standard Circular	Cleaneo	n/a	0.7	C	Perforated plasterboard with 200 mm cavity
Wall panels	Armstrong	Alphaclass	0.9	0.95	A	Mineral fiber wall panel
	Ecophon	Akusto Wall A	n/a	0.95	A	40 mm mineral fiber wall panel
	SoundSorba	WallSorba	0.95	0.9	A	40 mm fabric covered glass fiber core panel
	INC	Panl-Sorb PS-I-FS	0.9	n/a	A	Encapsulated metal panel industrial style
	Kinetics	HardSide Wall Panel	0.9	n/a	A	Fabric or vinyl finished fiber based wall panel
	Idealtec	Ideacustic 16	0.8	0.85	B	Timber wall panel on 50 mm cavity + 40 mm mineral fiber
	Icopal	Monafloor absorbent panel	0.9	0.85	B	50 mm fabric covered foam core panel

Category	Manufacturer	Product				Description
Spray plasters	CMS Danskin Oscar BASWA	Fellert Even Better	0.9	0.9	A	39 mm thick Scem/Sahara system
		Elite 25 mm	0.75	0.8	B	Spray on substrate 25 mm depth of system
		BASWAphon Classic Fine	0.75	n/a	n/a	30 mm classic fine finish
	Sto	Acoustic Spray Plaster	0.5	0.51	D	Spray plaster finish
Transparent panel absorbers	RPG	DeAmp Panel Absorber	0.5	0.5	D	4 mm perforated transparent sheet fixed in front of glazing unit
	RPG	DeAmp Double Panel	0.5	0.25	E	4 mm perforated transparent sheet fixed in front of glazing unit
Suspended systems	CEP	Sequence Acoustic Baffles	n/a	n/a/	A	Suspended horizontal or vertical fabric covered baffle
	Decoustics	Quadrillo	0.8	n/a	B	Suspended timber panel system
	H&H	HR Absorbers	n/a	0.56	C	Suspended horizontal colored fabric panel
	Ecophon	Solo Baffle c300	n/a	0.55	D	Suspended fabric faced mineral fiber baffle
Printed art panels	Soundsorba	Fotosorba	0.78	n/a	n/a	Digitally printed image on acoustic panel
	GIK	Acoustic ArPanel	n/a	n/a	n/a	Digitally printed image on acoustic panel

Table C.2 **Acoustic absorption performance levels of generic room finishes**

Standard room surfaces	NRC	α_w	Absorption class
6mm pile carpet on foam underlay	0.30–0.35	0.24–0.38	E
Brickwork	0.05	0.02–0.04	n/a
Carpet and underlay	0.55	0.4–0.5	D
Carpet tiles	n/a	0.4	D
Child	n/a	0.2–0.3	n/a
Concrete	0.05	0.02–0.04	n/a
Desk and chair	n/a	0.5	n/a
Dryline/plasterboard on dabs	n/a	0.02–0.04	n/a
Dryline/plasterboard on frame	0.05–0.1	0.05–0.1	n/a
Floorboards on joists	0.1	0.09	n/a
Glass	0.05–0.15	0.05–0.1	n/a
Marble	0	0.01	n/a
Parquet	0.05–0.10	0.12	n/a
Perforated metal ceiling tray with mineral fiber behind	n/a	0.3–0.7	D–C
Person	n/a	0.4	n/a
Plaster on block/brick	0.05	0.02–0.05	n/a
Rubber	0.05	0.05–0.07	n/a
Steel	0.1	0.07–0.10	n/a
Tiles	0.01	0.02	n/a
Timber doors	0.1	0.10–0.15	E
Upholstered seat	n/a	0.5–0.7	n/a
Vinyl on concrete	0.05	0.03	n/a
Water	0	0.01	n/a
Wood panels	0.01	0.1–0.2	E

C.2 Insulation

Wall type A

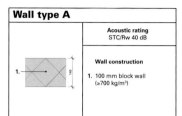

Acoustic rating
STC/Rw 40 dB

Wall construction

1. 100 mm block wall
   (≥700 kg/m³)

Wall type B

Acoustic rating
STC/Rw 40 dB

Wall construction

1. 100 mm block wall
   (≥700 kg/m³)

2. 8 mm sand/cement render

Wall type C

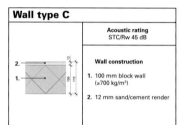

Acoustic rating
STC/Rw 45 dB

Wall construction

1. 100 mm block wall
   (≥700 kg/m³)

2. 12 mm sand/cement render

Wall type D

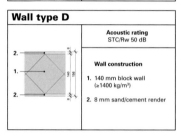

Acoustic rating
STC/Rw 50 dB

Wall construction

1. 140 mm block wall
   (≥1400 kg/m³)

2. 8 mm sand/cement render

Wall type E

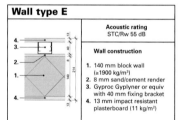

Acoustic rating
STC/Rw 55 dB

Wall construction

1. 140 mm block wall
   (≥1900 kg/m³)
2. 8 mm sand/cement render
3. Gyproc Gyplyner or equiv
   with 40 mm fixing bracket
4. 13 mm impact resistant
   plasterboard (11 kg/m²)

Wall type F

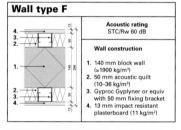

Acoustic rating
STC/Rw 60 dB

Wall construction

1. 140 mm block wall
   (≥1900 kg/m³)
2. 50 mm acoustic quilt
   (10–36 kg/m³)
3. Gyproc Gyplyner or equiv
   with 50 mm fixing bracket
4. 13 mm impact resistant
   plasterboard (11 kg/m²)

Wall type G

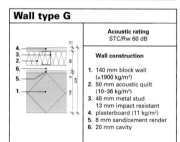

Acoustic rating
STC/Rw 60 dB

Wall construction

1. 140 mm block wall
   (≥1900 kg/m³)
2. 50 mm acoustic quilt
   (10–36 kg/m³)
3. 48 mm metal stud
   13 mm impact resistant
4. plasterboard (11 kg/m²)
5. 8 mm sand/cement render
6. 20 mm cavity

Wall type H

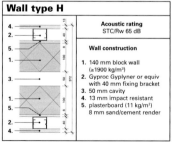

Acoustic rating
STC/Rw 65 dB

Wall construction

1. 140 mm block wall
   (≥1900 kg/m³)
2. Gyproc Gyplyner or equiv
   with 40 mm fixing bracket
3. 50 mm cavity
4. 13 mm impact resistant
5. plasterboard (11 kg/m²)
   8 mm sand/cement render

C.1 Masonry wall specifications

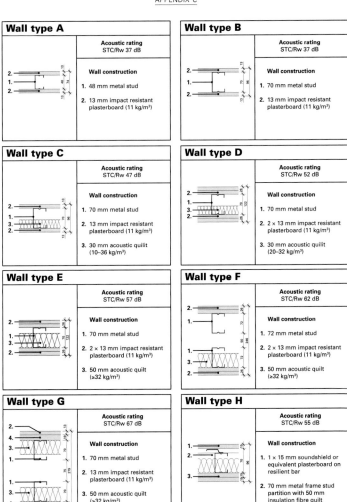

Wall type A

	Acoustic rating STC/Rw 37 dB
2. 1. 2.	**Wall construction** 1. 48 mm metal stud 2. 13 mm impact resistant plasterboard (11 kg/m³)

Wall type B

	Acoustic rating STC/Rw 37 dB
2. 1. 2.	**Wall construction** 1. 70 mm metal stud 2. 13 mm impact resistant plasterboard (11 kg/m³)

Wall type C

	Acoustic rating STC/Rw 47 dB
2. 1. 3. 2.	**Wall construction** 1. 70 mm metal stud 2. 13 mm impact resistant plasterboard (11 kg/m³) 3. 30 mm acoustic quilt (10–36 kg/m³)

Wall type D

	Acoustic rating STC/Rw 52 dB
2. 1. 3. 2.	**Wall construction** 1. 70 mm metal stud 2. 2 × 13 mm impact resistant plasterboard (11 kg/m³) 3. 30 mm acoustic quilit (20–32 kg/m³)

Wall type E

	Acoustic rating STC/Rw 57 dB
2. 1. 3. 2.	**Wall construction** 1. 70 mm metal stud 2. 2 × 13 mm impact resistant plasterboard (11 kg/m³) 3. 50 mm acoustic quilt (≥32 kg/m³)

Wall type F

	Acoustic rating STC/Rw 62 dB
2. 1. 1. 3. 2.	**Wall construction** 1. 72 mm metal stud 2. 2 × 13 mm impact resistant plasterboard (11 kg/m³) 3. 50 mm acoustic quilt (≥32 kg/m³)

Wall type G

	Acoustic rating STC/Rw 67 dB
2. 4. 3. 1. 1. 3. 4. 2.	**Wall construction** 1. 70 mm metal stud 2. 13 mm impact resistant plasterboard (11 kg/m³) 3. 50 mm acoustic quilt (≥32 kg/m³) 4. 19 mm plasterboard plank (14.5 kg/m³)

Wall type H

	Acoustic rating STC/Rw 55 dB
1. 2. 3.	**Wall construction** 1. 1 × 15 mm soundshield or equivalent plasterboard on resilient bar 2. 70 mm metal frame stud partition with 50 mm insulation fibre quilt 3. 2 × 15 soundshield or equivalent plasterboard

Note:
C-Studs may be replaced by I-section studs where necessary. If I-section studs are to be used, then the depth of the section must equal that of C-Stud.

C.2 Metal stud-wall specifications

Wall type A

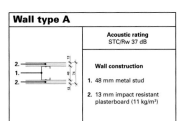

Acoustic rating
STC/Rw 37 dB

Wall construction

1. 48 mm metal stud

2. 13 mm impact resistant plasterboard (11 kg/m³)

Wall type B

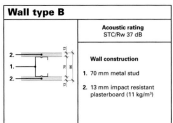

Acoustic rating
STC/Rw 37 dB

Wall construction

1. 70 mm metal stud

2. 13 mm impact resistant plasterboard (11 kg/m³)

Wall type C

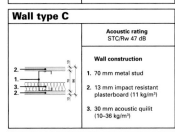

Acoustic rating
STC/Rw 47 dB

Wall construction

1. 70 mm metal stud

2. 13 mm impact resistant plasterboard (11 kg/m³)

3. 30 mm acoustic quilt (10–36 kg/m³)

Wall type D

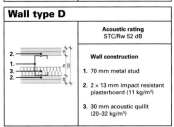

Acoustic rating
STC/Rw 52 dB

Wall construction

1. 70 mm metal stud

2. 2 × 13 mm impact resistant plasterboard (11 kg/m³)

3. 30 mm acoustic quilit (20–32 kg/m³)

Wall type E

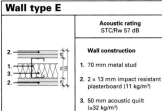

Acoustic rating
STC/Rw 57 dB

Wall construction

1. 70 mm metal stud

2. 2 × 13 mm impact resistant plasterboard (11 kg/m³)

3. 50 mm acoustic quilt (≥32 kg/m³)

Wall type F

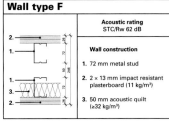

Acoustic rating
STC/Rw 62 dB

Wall construction

1. 72 mm metal stud

2. 2 × 13 mm impact resistant plasterboard (11 kg/m³)

3. 50 mm acoustic quilt (≥32 kg/m³)

Wall type G

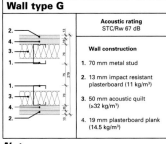

Acoustic rating
STC/Rw 67 dB

Wall construction

1. 70 mm metal stud

2. 13 mm impact resistant plasterboard (11 kg/m³)

3. 50 mm acoustic quilt (≥32 kg/m³)

4. 19 mm plasterboard plank (14.5 kg/m³)

Wall type H

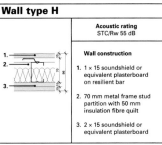

Acoustic rating
STC/Rw 55 dB

Wall construction

1. 1 × 15 soundshield or equivalent plasterboard on resilient bar

2. 70 mm metal frame stud partition with 50 mm insulation fibre quilt

3. 2 × 15 soundshield or equivalent plasterboard

Note:

C-Studs may be replaced by I-section studs where necessary. If I-section studs are to be used, then the depth of the section must equal that of C-Stud.

C.3 Timber stud-wall specifications

Hollow core floor slabs

PERFORMANCE
STC/Rw 55 dB

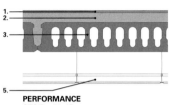

PERFORMANCE
STC/Rw 60 dB

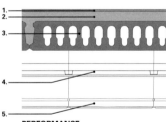

PERFORMANCE
STC/Rw 65 dB

CONSTRUCTION

1. Soft bonded carpet on vinyl floor finish min Δ Lw 18 dB
2. 50–75 mm floor screed
3. 200 mm minimum deep hollow core concrete floor slab (≥300 kg/m³)
4. Suspended metal frame plasterboard (≥11 kg/m³) ceiling
5. Suspended metal frame ceiling with mineral board ceiling tile

Steel composite floor decks

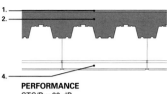

PERFORMANCE
STC/Rw 60 dB

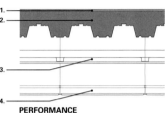

PERFORMANCE
STC/Rw 65 dB

CONSTRUCTION

1. Soft bonded carpet on vinyl floor finish min Δ Lw 18 dB
2. 175 mm minimum deep composite concrete floor slab (≥365 kg/m³)
4. Suspended metal frame plasterboard (≥11 kg/m³) ceiling
5. Suspended metal frame ceiling with mineral board ceiling tile

C.4 Masonry floor specifications

Index